BREAKING THE POWER OF LIMITATION

J. Larry Gunter

Breaking The Power Of Limitation
J Larry Gunter

ISBN - 978-1-329-49155-7

BREAKING THE POWER OF LIMITATION

DEDICATION

This book is dedicated to my beautiful wife Kathleen Gunter, who has stood by my side for many years as we travelled across the world preaching the gospel of Jesus Christ. I would also like to dedicate this book to Victorious Life Church. God has blessed me to pastor this wonderful congregation for the past 18 years. Victorious Life Church has provided me the time and opportunity to share my passion with many around the world.

I also want to express my appreciation to a very special person Annetta T. Swift, who was so instrumental in the processing of this book. On January 28th, 2015, I was preaching at Living Faith Tabernacle for Dr. Chris Bowen. The message that night was very prophetic. God allowed me to speak a prophetic word into Annetta Swift that in 6 months God was going to do an amazing thing in her life. Little did I know that she had a business called, In Other Words d/b/a The Ready Writer. It was through an email that Annetta T Swift sent me 6 months later informing me that God brought the prophecy to pass. Immediately, we knew this was a divine connection which would propel this book into a reality. She's is a playwright, author and the answer for my publishing needs. She comes highly recommended. Contact her for your publishing needs, special services or purchase one of her many books. www.thereadywriter.com

TABLE OF CONTENTS

FOREWORD
DR. CHRIS BOWEN

SENIOR PASTOR LIVING FAITH INTERNATIONAL MINISTRIES, FOREST PARK, GA

The Bible tells us that it rains on the just and the unjust. Christians are in no way exempt from seasons of storms, temptations or heartache. But just like natural disasters that take place in life, leaving devastation and destruction, what makes the difference in the rebuilding & recovery of the community is the attitude of those affected by the storm.

In his book, Breaking the Power of Limitation, Pastor Larry Gunter encourages and inspires the reader to not become a product of their environment or circumstances, but rather to rise above them and use the power God gives to make a positive impact on their world!

CHAPTER ONE

BREAKING THE YOKE OF LIMITATION

And it shall come to pass in that day, that his burden shall be taken away from off your shoulder, and his yoke from off your neck, and the yoke shall be destroyed because of the anointing.

— Isaiah 10:27

I believe that in every level and season of life there is an anointing or a blessing for that season. Not only are there levels and seasons, but God has grace for those levels and seasons of your life – even if it's a season that you don't want to be in at that time.

THE REASON YOU ARE ABLE TO GET THROUGH DIFFICULT SEASONS IN YOUR LIFE IS BECAUSE GOD GIVES YOU A GRACE FOR THAT SEASON!

That grace or blessing was the very thing that provoked your praise to rise up within you during your difficult season. When you look back on those difficult times in your life, you begin to realize that had it not been for The Lord who was on your side, you would never have been able to make it through those dark times.

And Esau said to his father, "Have you but one blessing, my father? Bless me, even me also, O my father." And Esau lifted up his voice, and wept. And Isaac his father answered and said to him, "Behold, your dwelling shall be the fatness of the earth, and of the dew of heaven from above; And by your sword shall you live, and shall serve your brother; and it shall come to pass when you shall have the dominion, that you shall break his yoke from off your neck."

— Genesis 27:38-40

In Genesis 27, we find Esau going to his father to receive his blessing. Esau represents the person who has missed his grace or blessing. Esau missed the season he was supposed to be in at this time in his life. The Bible says that Esau and Jacob knew that their father Isaac was an old man and near death. They also knew that Isaac would pronounce his final blessing on the oldest son, as was the custom in that day.

As the years progressed, Isaac became old and his health began to deteriorate; he was about 130 years old at this time. We calculate this age by noting that Jacob was 130 when he entered the land of Egypt (Genesis 47:9). Joseph (Jacob's son) was approximately 44 at that time (Genesis 41:46). Joseph was born after Jacob had worked 14 years for his wives (Genesis 30:25; 31:28). Subtracting these ages out, it would mean Jacob was about 70 when he left home. Since Jacob was born when Isaac was 60, it means that Isaac at this time is about 130. Isaac's eyesight had become so bad that he could not see. His sense of taste was also poor. As we will see shortly, he could not even distinguish between how goat and venison tasted.

Isaac was determined to give Esau, the oldest twin, the family blessing before his death. The blessing was the right to become the head of the family after the death of the father. Unfortunately, Isaac was attempting to go against God's will. The prophecy given to his wife Rebekah before the birth of Esau and Jacob stated that Jacob would be the ruling son. In addition, Esau had shown himself to be an immoral and careless man. Esau was so reckless that he sold half of his inheritance to his brother for a bowl of bean soup. Surely, Esau was not the best choice for the blessing.

However, looking closely at the story, we see that Isaac's mind is made up. To mark the occasion, Isaac orders Esau to prepare a feast from the game he has hunted. Rebekah happens to overhear Isaac's plans for Esau. It appears Isaac has been secretive about his plans, since he did not tell Rebekah about them. Perhaps he knew she would have objected, so he avoided the confrontation all together.

Rebekah then lays her own plans to interfere with Isaac's plans. She should have left matters in God's hands, as God is able to carry out

His own will in all matters. However, Rebekah tells Jacob to butcher two young goats, which she then prepares in a way that Isaac particularly likes.

At first, Jacob is reluctant to go along with his mother's scheme. He points out that even though Isaac is blind, he could still tell the difference between his sons by their hairiness. If Isaac realizes he is being fooled, he would pronounce a curse on Jacob instead of a blessing. However, Rebekah says if a curse is given, it would be on her for designing a scheme that failed.

Jacob eventually obeys his mother. Rebekah dresses Jacob in Esau's clothing and uses the skins from the goats on the backs of Jacob's hands and around his neck so Jacob will feel hairy like his brother. Jacob brings the food to Isaac and announces that he is Esau. This of course is a deliberate lie and he is almost found out immediately. Something doesn't sit right with Isaac; perhaps he realizes it is too soon for Esau to return, or perhaps the voice is not quite right. He checks his son's hands and smells his clothing and Isaac decides Jacob feels and smells like Esau. Isaac then proceeds to give Jacob the blessing.

However, we must understand that what Isaac had originally planned was in direct opposition to God's earlier statement in Genesis 25:23. Look carefully at Isaac's statement in Genesis 27:29. If this was given to Esau instead of Jacob, it would have been the opposite of God's prophecy!

Esau comes in shortly after Jacob leaves. It does not take Isaac long to realize what happened. The emotions rack him so strongly that he begins to shake. He realizes that despite his plans to defeat God's plans, God manages to get His way anyway. As Paul later states: "God is able to make all things to work for the good of His people" (Romans 8:28). This even includes the sins of other people.

Esau howls in anger and begs for a blessing from Isaac, but no amount of begging can change the past. Isaac will not change what God has obviously intended to occur. As it often happens, an angry person will blame everything that happens on anyone but himself. Esau claims it is in Jacob's character to deceive people. The truth is that only Jacob's *name* means deceiver. Jacob is a reluctant participant in these events. Esau also claims that Jacob stole his birthright. However, the truth is that Esau sold it to Jacob for a bowl of bean soup. Esau also claims that Jacob stole his blessing. However, the blessing was not his in the first place since God had already proclaimed it belonged to Jacob. How can someone steal what is already his?

The story of Esau is one that repeats in modern life. A young person, raised by Christians, rebels against all he is taught. He fills his life with the fleeting pleasures of the world and then is shocked when he reaps a harvest of pain and woe.

Isaac does manage to provide a small blessing on Esau's behalf. Esau's descendants would dwell in a rugged country, away from the fatness of the land and the dew of heaven promised to Jacob. His descendants would spend much of their time in warfare. They would serve Jacob's descendants as promised to Jacob. (This was fulfilled when Edom was conquered by David and was placed in subjection to Israel.) However, Isaac offers one glimmer of hope – they would break their yoke one day.

Esau was the oldest son and being the oldest son he was entitled to the father's blessing, but Esau will miss the blessing for that season.

And Esau said to his father, "Have you but one blessing, my father? Bless me, even me also, O my father." And Esau lifted up his voice, and wept. And Isaac his father answered and said to him, "Behold, your dwelling shall be the fatness of the earth, and of the dew of heaven from above; And by your sword shall you live, and shall

serve your brother; and it shall come to pass when you shall have the dominion, that you shall break his yoke from off your neck."
— Genesis 27:38-40

Now notice how Esau comes back to his father after missing the blessing and asks his father Isaac, "Have you but one blessing, my father? Bless me, even me also, O my father." And Esau lifted up his voice, and wept. In other words, Esau is asking, "Father is there only one blessing? Is there not another one? Is this the only season I get?" When Esau looks back on his season to be blessed, and misses his blessing, he begins to question where he is. Is there not another blessing? The ability to judge, the ability to see where you are, and the ability to understand what season of your life that you are in right now is critical. If you can't discern where you are in life, or what season you are in right now, you can miss the blessing and feel like there are no more blessings left for you.

For example, when the Children of Israel went through the land, God would not allow them to go through the land any old way they decided to travel. God would not allow them to go through the land without a particular order. God had them place the Ark of the Covenant in the center of the tribes as they marched through the land. There were tribes to the north, south, east, and west, with the ark of the covenant in the middle of the twelve tribes. An aerial view of them marching looked like a cross moving through the wilderness.
Now notice this, the first tribe to move into the land and walk through it was the tribe of Judah. Judah always goes first. The tribe of Judah was descended from the patriarch Judah, the fourth son of Jacob and Leah, and the name *Judah* means "praise" or "to praise" as revealed in Genesis 29:35 (NIV). "She conceived again, and when she gave birth to a son she said, 'This time I will praise the Lord.' " So she named him *Judah*.

When we move from season to the next season, or from one level to the next level in life, the first thing we should go into that next

season or level of life with is Praise! Praise is the power that allows us to enter into a season of life that we haven't figured out yet.
When we pray, we should begin with praise and end with praise. The Lord's prayer gives us this example and Philippians 4:6-7 tells us, "Be careful for nothing; but in everything by prayer and supplication with thanksgiving let your requests be made known unto God. And the peace of God, which passeth all understanding, shall keep your hearts and minds through Christ Jesus."

When you pray with thanksgiving, the peace of God will keep your heart and mind. The Apostle Paul was persecuted and suffered far more than most of us, yet he put it all in perspective in 2 Corinthians 4:17-18: "For our light affliction, which is but for a moment, works for us a far more exceeding and eternal weight of glory; While we look not at the things which are seen, but at the things which are not seen: for the things which are seen are temporal; but the things which are not seen are eternal." First, Paul said our affliction is just for a moment in light of eternity; he looked into the spiritual realm. Praise will push you into the spiritual realm to see what God has done for you. Paul and Silas praised God in prison and it was praise that released the power of God and caused the earthquake that delivered them from their captivity.

Praise will build you up spiritually and keep you from crumbling, "For the joy of the LORD is your strength" (Nehemiah 8:10). However, praising God doesn't just affect us; it is a powerful weapon against the devil as well. Psalm 8:2 says, "Out of the mouth of babes and sucklings hast thou ordained strength because of thine enemies, that thou mightest still the enemy and the avenger." In Matthew 21:16, at the time of his triumphal entry into Jerusalem (Palm Sunday), Jesus quotes from Psalm 8, and He interchanges the words *perfected praise* with *ordained strength*. This is a tremendous revelation: Praise is strength (Nehemiah 8:10)!

Praise will lead and guide you through unpredictable seasons of life. Do you know that praising God is the best thing to do first, before doing anything else? Have you ever been in a situation where you feel all alone? Or have you encountered a difficult situation in your life and you didn't know what to do, like losing your job or suffering the loss of someone very close to your heart? Consider good times, like receiving a raise from your boss or earning high marks at school. What do you usually do during these moments? Praising God makes every circumstance of our lives complete, essential, and eminently worthwhile.

Webster defines the word *praise* this way: "to say good things about something or someone," and it is synonymous to words such as admire, commend, extol, honor, and worship. A Christian definition of *praise* is: "the joyful thanking and adoring of God; the celebration of His goodness and grace."

Why is praising God important? The reasons are countless. First and foremost, God deserves to be praised and He is worthy to receive our praise:

For great is the LORD and most worthy of praise; he is to be feared above all gods.

— Psalm 96:4

Great is the LORD and most worthy of praise; his greatness no one can fathom.

— Psalm 145:3

I call to the LORD, who is worthy of praise, and I am saved from my enemies.

— 2 Samuel 22:4

You are worthy, our LORD and God, to receive glory and honor and power, for you created all things, and by your will they were created and have their being.

— Revelation 4:11

Praising God is useful and favorable for us. By praising God, we are reminded of the greatness of God! His power and presence in our lives is reinforced in our understanding. “Praise the Lord, for the Lord is good; sing praise to his name, for that is pleasant” (Psalm 135:3).

Praise discharges strength in faith, which causes God to move on our behalf: “From the lips of children and infants you have ordained praise because of your enemies, to silence the foe and the avenger” (Psalm 8:2). Praising God also transforms the spiritual environment around us. In 2 Chronicles 5:13-14, the alteration that happened when the Levites gave praise and thanks to the Lord is clearly illustrated as the temple was filled with a cloud, signifying the glory of God. “The trumpeters and singers joined in unison, as with one voice, to give praise and thanks to the LORD. Accompanied by trumpets, cymbals, and other instruments, they raised their voices in praise to the LORD and sang: ‘He is good; his love endures forever.’ Then the temple of the LORD was filled with a cloud, and the priests could not perform their service because of the cloud, for the glory of the LORD filled the temple of God.”

God inhabits the atmosphere of praise. Psalm 22:3 (KJV) says, “But thou art holy, O thou that inhabits the praises of Israel.” If we want to see a clear manifestation of God's blessings and grace, all we need to do is to praise Him with all our heart, our mind, and our soul.

Who is to praise God?

Let everything that has breath praise the LORD. Praise the LORD.
— Psalm 150:6.

I will extol the LORD at all times; his praise will always be on my lips.
— Psalm 34:1

Because your love is better than life, my lips will glorify you. I will praise you as long as I live, and in your name I will lift up my hands.
— Psalm 63:3-4

Praise the LORD, all you servants of the LORD who minister by night in the house of the LORD. Lift up your hands in the sanctuary and praise the LORD.

— Psalm 134:1-2

We cannot enjoy the true joy and benefits of praising God until we have received Jesus Christ as our Lord and Savior. As children of God, He dwells in our bodies through the Holy Spirit. This means that wherever we go, God is to be praised. In 1 Corinthians 6:19-20 it states, "Do you not know that your body is a temple of the Holy Spirit, who is in you, whom you have received from God? You are not your own; you were bought at a price. Therefore honor God with your body."

How do we praise God?

How can we actually praise God? Singing songs and hymns, clapping our hands, even jumping for joy, are options, but the list is endless. We can give glory and praise to our God with the use of our physical bodies, with our hearts and minds, and with our deeds. There are many ways to praise God! No matter how you choose to praise and worship God, it should result in awe of God's power, love, and grace for all of us!

WE CAN PRAISE OUR WAY INTO A NEW SEASON!

Judah which means "praise" was always first. The tribe Dan was always last. Dan represents "keen judgment." Dan or the spirit of discernment must walk through that same season that our praise has led us through. Dan, or "keen judgment," comes behind our season of praise to judge or question where we have been.

In other words…

1. What did I learn in this lesson or season of life?

2. What blessing did I miss in this season?

3. What distracted me in this season?

4. What mistakes did I make in this season?

The lesson is this: if you don't learn what mistakes you made, then you are destined to repeat the same mistakes again and again in life.

Praise will get you from one season to the next season, but you still need the spirit of discernment to reveal to you what you missed in that season or what you learned from that season. Because if you can't look behind you and see where you've been or discern where you are going, you will find yourself walking around in circles.

THERE IS A BIG DIFFERENCE IN WALKING AND POSSESSING!

You can walk around in circles, but never possess the land. You can walk around in circles and never possess the place or the promise you walked on. You can praise your way in circles, but never possess anything your praise is talking about.

YOU CAN PRAISE GOD ABOUT GOING TO THE OTHER SIDE AND NEVER GET TO THE OTHER SIDE.

- You can sing songs about "He has made me glad," but leave church mad!
- You can shout the praise that "God is good all the time, and all the time God is good," but walk out of your house saying, "God doesn't care about me!"
- It's possible to say, "I will bless God at all times," but live a defeated and depressed life.
- It's possible to talk faith at church, but get home from church and confess doubt and unbelief.

Esau realized he missed the blessing because:

- He got distracted.
- He was careless.
- He was more focused on the appetite of the flesh than on the reward of the future.

WHAT HAS CAUSED YOU TO MISS YOUR BLESSING?

There are many reasons why you may miss your blessing. Did you know that the pain of a previous season can cause you to miss the blessing? You can miss your season of blessing by your inability to judge where you are in life. You can miss your season by allowing people to define your abilities for you, rather than listening to what God says. You can also miss your season by a lack of confidence in the anointing or grace that is on your life.

Esau went back to his father and desperately asked, **"IS THERE NOT ANOTHER BLESSING FOR ME?" "DON'T I GET ANOTHER CHANCE?" "DON'T I GET ANOTHER SEASON TO BE BLESSED?"** According to Genesis 27:38-40:

v. 38: Esau said to his father, "Do you have only one blessing, my father? Bless me too, my father!" Then Esau wept aloud.

v. 39: His father Isaac answered him, "Your dwelling will be away from the earth's richness, away from the dew of heaven above.

v. 40: You will live by the sword and you will serve your brother. But when you grow restless, you will throw his yoke from off your neck."

In other words, Isaac was telling Esau, "If you remain at this level or season of life, your blessing will be limited and you will live the rest of your life away from the dew of heaven."

The phrase, "dew of Heaven" is mentioned in seven verses of scripture in the Bible and implies "the abundant blessings of God!"

In verse 40, Isaac tells Esau, "You will live by the sword and you will serve your brother. But when you grow restless, you will throw his yoke from off your neck." In other words, You will live by the sword and you will have to fight for every blessing you get. You will have to not only fight for every blessing you get, but you will have to fight to keep that blessing.

The second thing Isaac says is, "You will serve your brother." You will never feel like you are appreciated. You will always struggle to get ahead. You will never be able to get to where you know you need to be. You will always feel like somebody just keeps pushing you back.

IT DOESN'T HAVE TO BE THAT WAY!

Verse 40 also says, "But when you grow restless, you will throw his yoke from off your neck." The reason you feel this way at times (restless) is because you have a yoke around your neck. These yokes are so restrictive that when placed on oxen, the oxen were unable to turn their heads left or right. The only direction they can move their heads in these yokes is in an up and down motion.

Here is what Isaac was saying to Esau: "NOT ONLY WILL THE BLESSING BE LIMITED AND YOU WILL STRUGGLE TO GET A BLESSING AND KEEP IT, **BUT YOU WILL BE SO BOUND THAT ALL YOU CAN DO IS AGREE WITH YOUR OPPRESSION.** You will be put into a position of agreement with the enemy. When you nod your head up or down in agreement to whatever the enemy says, he has a yoke around your neck.

- You will agree with your discouragement
- You will agree with your pain
- You will agree with your circumstance

YOU WON'T HAVE THE ABILITY TO SAY NO, BUT WHEN YOU FINALLY GROW RESTLESS, YOU CAN BREAK THAT YOKE.

The Five Stages of a Restless Spirit:

1. Restlessness begins with discontentment.

At some point in life, you must become dissatisfied with where you are in life. Things may not change in one day but things will eventually change. When you grow restless in your spirit, that's the beginning of discontentment. Nothing changes as long as you are content with way things are.

2. Nothing will happen until you become discontented with where you are in life.

If the enemy can persuade you to be content with where you are in life, he can cause you to lose your fight. He wants you to accept where you are and call it normal, because if you accept it as being normal, you can't be delivered from it. What you tolerate, you become use to. What you tolerate, you won't fix. What you become used to, you never see any need to change. You will accept it until somebody begins to question it.

Discontentment produces questions:

- Why am I feeling this way?
- Why can't I get ahead?
- Why am I always struggling?
- Why is my life so messed up?

AS LONG AS YOU ARE SATISFIED WITH THE STATUS QUO, THINGS WILL REMAIN THE SAME AND NEVER CHANGE.

3. Questions will produce new revelations or options.

The four men who sat outside the gate of Samaria didn't see any options or have a revelation for better until they started to question,

"Why sit we here until we die?" They reasoned with themselves, If we stay here, we will die. **However, if we move from here and head to the enemy's camp, they may feed us and let us live.**

4. New revelations lead to new beliefs.

When you have a revelation that things can be better, you will start believing differently about your future. If God ever works a miracle in your life or turn some things around, you begin believing differently about God.

5. New beliefs will produce new actions.

When Esau believed he could be blessed, his actions began to change. Remember when Esau was hungry, Jacob fed him stew. Esau had been out in the field hunting for meat, but Jacob didn't have to go hunting for it; Jacob was raising livestock at home. So what and why was Esau out hunting?

Eventually the day came when Esau gets another blessing. Esau and Jacob are about to meet again after years of hate between them. Jacob is afraid of Esau because Esau had threatened to kill him. Jacob sends Esau herds of livestock as a peace offering. However, Esau sends word back to Jacob, "I don't need your herds because I have herds of my own." Genesis 33:9 details this: "But Esau said, 'I already have plenty, my brother. Keep what you have for yourself.' "

ESAU'S FIRST BLESSING CAME BY BIRTH AND HE MISSED IT, BUT THE SECOND BLESSING CAME BY DELIBERATE ORDER.

When you become restless and stop accepting where you are, you will break the yoke:

- You stop living in agreement with your circumstances.
- You stop agreeing with your poverty.
- You stop agreeing with your pain.

Break This Yoke in Jesus' Name!

According to Isaiah 10:27, "And it shall come to pass in that day, that his burden shall be taken away from off your shoulder, and his yoke from off your neck, and the yoke shall be destroyed because of the anointing." What does the original Hebrew say? To put it in Hebrew-English, the text reads, "The yoke shall be destroyed because of shamen" (pronounced SHA-MEN). What does the word *shamen* mean? The KJV translators understood it to be the equivalent of *shemen oil*, which apparently led them to think of oil for anointing, and then to the anointing itself. This is obviously quite a leap – really, an impossible leap – and there is nowhere in the Hebrew Bible where the word *shemen oil* by itself means "anointing." (For those with little or no Hebrew background, it was fine for the KJV translators to equate *shamen* with *shemen*; they simply erred when they translated it to mean "anointing.")

What then, is the text actually saying? It's best to understand *shamen* here to mean "fatness" (pronounced SHA-MEYN), which would produce a literal translation of: "The yoke will be destroyed because of the FAT."

BUT WHAT DOES THAT ACTUALLY MEAN?

The New International Version expresses it well: "In that day their burden will be lifted from your shoulders, their yoke from your neck; the yoke will be broken because you have grown so fat."

NOW PICTURE THIS: Here is an ox with a yoke on its neck, enslaving the ox to the will of its master, forcing it into a life of servitude. Eventually, however, it gets so healthy and fat that the yoke simply bursts from off its neck. That ox is now free!

And that is a picture for each of us when we find ourselves bound or oppressed or beaten into submission by the enemy. We simply feed our spirits the living Word day and night, we continue in worship, praise, prayer, and communion, and little by little, we get so healthy and strong – so *FAT* – that suddenly the yoke of oppression has to burst. ***THE FATNESS OF THE WORD OF GOD DESTROYS THE YOKE!***

IT'S TIME TO BREAK THE YOKES!

His father Isaac answered him; "Your dwelling will be away from the earth's riches, away from the dew of heaven above. You will live by the sword and you will serve your brother. But when you grow restless, you will break his yoke from off your neck."

— Genesis 27:29-30

Many people like Esau have had a life programmed for difficulties. They have yokes placed on their shoulders, thus there is a limit they can't go beyond. This can be caused by unbroken curses, and they need to break the yokes binding them before they can cancel any curse spoken against them. Anytime they want to break through they find it difficult. They have yokes of limitation placed in their way by the devil in the spiritual realm. Their lives are characterized by lack, pain, fear, hopelessness, poverty, disease, failure, etc. Many have tried to break through but have failed, while others have broken free. You don't have to be yoked with this. Esau was told the secret of breaking free from this yoke by his father— he had to be tired of it and grow restless.

You should be restless until your heaven opens. Arise and ask the Lord to reveal to you the yokes in your life, and break them in Jesus' name. Speak to every yoke, early in the morning, during the day, and even at night. Demand that every yoke be broken. Mention the yoke by name and persist in your prayers till dew from heaven relocates you.

BEGIN TO PRAY THIS PRAYER NOW IN JESUS' NAME!

You, yoke of defeat over my life, break in Jesus' name. I command the yoke of fear to break in Jesus' name. I break every yoke of limitation in my life in pieces in Jesus' name. I command every invisible yoke in my life to catch fire and burn to nothingness in Jesus' name. Lord, anoint me with the anointing that breaks every yoke of the enemy. I break loose today from the yoke of lack (mention any other yokes that you feel led to) *in Jesus' name. I will not be yoked together with demons of lust, defeat, fear* (state what you think is binding you). *I break this yoke now in Jesus' name. I release myself to unlimited divine breakthroughs in Jesus' name! Amen!*

DON'T GIVE UP—REMEMBER TO P.U.S.H.!
Pray Until Something Happens.

THE BREAKING OF YOUR YOKE WILL SET YOU FREE TO YOUR DIVINE BREAKTHROUGHS, IN JESUS' NAME.

CHAPTER TWO

PULLING UP STAKES THAT HOLD AND LIMIT US

If we accept the restraints that dictate what we can't do or can't be, then we will only know those things that are impossible with man, and never know what is possible with God.

Pulling Up Stakes

Many times in your pursuit of reaching your full potential and walking in your destiny, you come up against limitations. These limitations are either people-imposed or self-imposed. Let me explain. In life, you experience times of success and times of failure. Whether they are small or large, these experiences make an impact on your life. When you try to do something and fail, it is easy to make a decision to avoid that in the future. Automatically, you have enforced a self-imposed limitation in an area of your life that will affect your future success. Limitations can also be imposed by people who try to tie you down by saying, “You can't do that!” or “I can't see you in that role.” Whether these limitations are self-imposed or people-imposed, you must realize that they make a difference in how you see yourself. These are like small stakes in the soil of your mind that needlessly hold you back from reaching your full potential.

In order for you to move toward becoming the person God created you to be and fulfill the purpose He created you to fulfill, you must pull up these stakes and refuse to let limitations define you. What does the word *limitation* mean?

1. To be confined
2. To restrict
3. To keep within certain bounds
4. To restrain

For example, a circus elephant is often restricted by a stake and chain that seem to work in stopping it from walking free. This is achieved through chaining the elephant to a small steel stake from its youth. Once the baby elephant realizes that it can't break free, it never forgets that limitation. Hence, a six-ton elephant will not attempt to pull up its stake because of a stronghold that was formed in it from youth. This began with one thought that stays with the elephant for the rest of its life.

One thought can shape a person's destiny:

1. A thought produces an attitude.
2. An attitude produces behavioral patterns.
3. Behavioral patterns form character.
4. Character produces destiny.

Key: There is only one thing that limits the six-ton elephant from getting where he wants to go, and it's not a three-foot stake; it's a thought.

Attitudes are formed from a young age through various experiences that a child encounters in his or her life. From day one, school life has an enormous effect on the way many mature adults think today. Many teachers enforce wrong ways of thinking through their negative responses to a child's behavior in a classroom. Some teachers have been used by Satan to wrongly impart negative ways of thinking in a child's mind. These attitudes enforce restrictions in the life of the pupil. Behavioral patterns stem from the way an individual thinks. Our responses to good or bad situations are a direct result of the strongholds that have been formed in our minds.

Gideon as an Example

The Lord said two powerful things to Gideon while He was in the process of activating Gideon's potential to impact the nation of Israel in a righteous way. The first was: "The Lord is with you, you mighty man of valor" (Judges 6:12). And the second thing was: "Go in this might of yours" (Judges 6:14).

God spoke to activate and release the greatness in Gideon's life. God does not look at your weaknesses or past failures before using your life mightily. Gideon had an inferiority complex; the image he had of himself caused him to remain restricted from advancing into his maximum potential. Before Gideon could walk in his destiny, God had to upgrade the image he had of himself and the image he had of God.

Likewise God will strengthen the image you have of yourself, by revealing a deeper side of His character and ability to you, so that you are able to truly fulfill His plan for your life. This will happen throughout the course of your life and ministry through designated times and seasons appointed by the Lord. An example of this can be found in the life of Abraham. Over a period of twenty-five years, the Lord visited Abraham on several occasions to build in him a stronger image of his ability in the Lord. From the time God called Abraham out in Genesis 12, through to the fulfillment of Isaac's birth, the Lord chose specific seasons to visit Abraham in order to strengthen the image he had of God.

Although Abraham is recorded as one of the patriarchs of faith, he often struggled with the idea of the promise God made to him: "I will make you a great nation; I will bless you and make your name great" (Genesis 12:2). The Lord had to build into Abraham's heart and mind an image of what the Lord was able to do through him. God did this by replacing old thoughts and imaginations with new ones. Likewise, the Lord desires to replace old mentalities with new ones in order to free you to fulfill the plans of the Lord. "I can do all things through Christ who strengthens me" (Philippians 4:13).

Breaking limitations happens as we unbolt our minds from our inabilities and fasten our thoughts onto the greatness of our God! It only takes one thought to begin the process of restricting our lives from walking in the greatness God has destined for us. As the old saying goes, "A little leaven leavens the whole lump." Sow a habit and reap a destiny.

Renewing the Mind

Do not be conformed to this world but be transformed by the renewing of your mind.

— Romans 12:2

Transformation only takes place in the life of a believer as you identify the areas where you are being fashioned after the world's influences. The word *conform* means "to fashion one thing like another." In other words, you must stop talking like the world, acting like the world, and thinking like the world. This transformation will take place as you renew the way you think.

Renewing the mind is a lifelong journey for all that desire to walk in the perfect will of God. Even though you may be a Christian, this does not mean that you are walking free from the dictates of things such as fear, failure, discouragement, etc. To be transformed is to go through a complete change in form or kind.

The Greek word used in this verse is *metamorpho*. It means "to go through a complete change in form," such as the caterpillar does when it comes out of its cocoon as a butterfly. It doesn't just add some wings to its furry, long body; it completely changes into a different kind of being that can do totally different things and live a totally different life. This is true for the life of a Christian once his or her mind is renewed by the word of God.

Renewing the mind requires that we make a conscious effort and work at the following:

1. Be aware of how you really think.
2. Be willing to change your thought life.
3. Find out the way God thinks about you.

4. Meditate on the way God thinks about you.
5. Walk in the power of those thoughts in your everyday life.

By using this process in your daily life, thoughts that were once contrary to the Word of God will slowly decrease over a matter of time. This will not be instantaneous, it takes persistence and the anointing of God's word to slowly reinforce a completely new way of thinking.

Control Your Mind and You Will Walk in Your Destiny

For the weapons of our warfare are not carnal but mighty in God for the pulling down of strongholds, casting down arguments and every high thing that exalts itself against the knowledge of God, bringing every thought into captivity to the obedience of Christ.

— 2 Corinthians 10:4-5

The apostle Paul reveals one of the most important insights into spiritual warfare you need to understand. The mind is Satan's primary target; he knows that if he can cause a person to think a certain way, he has some form of control over them. Jesus has defeated demons and their power and given you the victory. However, you must appropriate this victory by controlling negative thoughts that can fill your mind and control your life. Paul says there are strongholds that take root in the mind that must be brought down. The word *stronghold* is a military term that describes a fortified place, or place of domination and control.

Keys to follow in overcoming wrong thoughts:

1. Identify the wrong thought.
2. Put it in its place.
3. Replace the thought with God's thought.
4. Your mind is the control center of your of your life

"For those who live according to the flesh set their minds on the things of the flesh, but those who live according to the Spirit, the things of the Spirit. For to be carnally minded is death, but to be spiritually minded is life and peace" (Romans 8:5-6).

- **Set your mind**: The word *set* means "to put in a specified place or position." Where your mind is set will determine whether you walk in the flesh or the Spirit.

If you set your mind on wrong things, eventually you will practice those things on which your mind is set.

Spiritually Minded

This position is attained when you are able to control your thoughts by setting your mind towards the things of God. By doing this you allow your spirit, along with the Holy Spirit, to position you to live a spirit-controlled life. Set your mind on things above and not on the things of the earth (Colossians 3:2). You make the choices in life to allow your mind to think on carnal thoughts or spiritual thoughts. Your feet will follow the path your mind has taken.

Therefore, gird up the loins of your mind, be sober and rest your hope fully upon the grace that is to be brought to you at the revelation of Jesus Christ.

—1Peter 1:13

The mind can take on a carnal mentality or a spiritual mentality (Romans 8:6-7). In order to abolish negative thoughts, you must adapt the tedious process of casting down arguments and every high thing that exalts itself against the knowledge of God and bringing every thought into captivity to the obedience of Christ (2 Corinthians 10:5). You must learn to replace wrong thoughts with right thoughts, and wrong imaginations with right imaginations.

Understanding Your Mind

In order to understand how the mind works, you need to look at some Greek words that will shed light on the function of your mind. There are three Greek words used in the New Testament for mind: ***Nous***, ***Phroneo***, and ***Dianoia***.

1. ***Nous*** and ***Phroneo*** belong to the fundamental part of the mind. ***Nous*** refers to the faculty of mental perception, understanding, and judgment. It is the processing faculty of the mind, similar to the CPU (central processing unit) of a computer system (Romans 14:5; 1 Corinthians 1:10), and it has the ability to have logical conviction (Romans 14:5). If you find yourself reasoning through everything, you are strong in this part of your mind. This part of your mind, however, can become the target of the enemy. He can cause you to become too logical in all of your reasoning, processing, and analyzing of everything (2 Thessalonians 2:2).

2. ***Phroneo*** literally means to be minded in a certain way. This part of your mind forms a mentality or mindset, like a computer software program (Romans 8:5; 2 Corinthians 10:5). Those who are caught in the web of traditional mindsets are often very strong-willed and are very hard to change. This part of your mind is trained to think a certain way (Galatians 5:10; 1 Peter 3:8).

3. ***Dianoia*** refers to thinking through. It is the deeper part of your mind—your imagination (Matthew 22:37; Mark12:30). It is the place where the Word of God can take root (2 Peter 3:10. You are instructed to keep this part of your mind fully alert (1 Peter 1:13). The imagination is very powerful in that it holds creative force. It can be likened to the picture factory of your mind.

Developing a Breakthrough Mentality

A mentality is a mindset, a pattern of thinking, or a way of seeing things. To have a breakthrough mentality is to prevail through barriers that seem impenetrable. These barriers only have their existence because you have given them power through meditating upon them. You must realize that we all meditate (to think something over continuously) day and night. By meditating upon the Word of God, you are actively replacing wrong thoughts with right ones that will help you to be fruitful in your life.

One of the major hindrances to breaking through into new things is your thinking pattern. Habits are slowly formed by ways of thinking. People often forget that to effectively walk free from old habits, you must replace those habits with new healthy habits. Changing old habits begins with changing old thoughts. By setting your mind towards right things, you are effectively opening up your heart to right things.

All of us need to break free from old thought patterns. People can live with wrong patterns of thought for years and not be aware of the strongholds they are living with on a daily basis. Being exposed to the anointing helps to bring light to these thought patterns. Human words will not break people free from ways of thinking; it takes the anointing of God upon your words to destroy these negative seeds. Wrong thoughts are negative seeds; if they are not aborted they will produce offspring. Wrong thoughts are like stakes in the soil of our minds; they must be pulled up in order for us to advance into new ground.

Common Stakes in Peoples' Lives

- Fear of failure
- Fear of the unknown
- Fear of man
- I can't do that
- I've never done it before

These are just some of the common thoughts you must deal with in order to break free from being restrained by wrong patterns of thought.

As a Man Thinks

Do not eat the bread of a miser, nor desire his delicacies; for as he thinks in his heart, so is he. "Eat and drink!" he says to you. But his heart is not with you.

— Proverbs 23:6-7

You are today what you thought yesterday, and tomorrow you will become what you think today.

A Sound Mind Produces a Sound Lifestyle

He replied, "Because you have so little faith. Truly I tell you, if you have faith as small as a mustard seed, you can say to this mountain, 'Move from here to there,' and it will move. Nothing will be impossible for you." When they came together in Galilee, he said to them, "The Son of Man is going to be delivered into the hands of men. They will kill him, and on the third day he will be raised to life." And the disciples were filled with grief.

— Mark 7:20-23

One of the keys to having a sound life is developing a sound mind. Eventually, what is stored in your mind will make its way out of your mouth. It only takes the right situations to reveal what is truly in your heart. Things such as outbursts of anger and wrath are a result of negative thoughts that have become ungodly strongholds in your mind. Before a person commits the act of murder, he or she spends time thinking over and meditating upon negative thoughts. These thoughts empower a person to respond by acting out the very issue that his or her mind was set upon.

Progress Begins with a Thought

Now Jabez was more honorable than his brothers, and his mother called his name Jabez, saying, "Because I bore him in pain." And Jabez called on the God of Israel saying, "Oh that you would bless me indeed and enlarge my territory, that your hand would be with me, and that you would keep me from evil, that I may not cause pain!" So God granted him what he requested.

— 1 Chronicles 4:9-10

These two verses of scripture are key examples of a man who chose to break free from the reproach over his life. The name *Jabez* basically means "pain." His name reflected the reproach he carried in his heart, "one that brings pain." Jabez could have settled to live with this stronghold all of his life. However, he chose to break free from the state that he was in by asking the Lord to transform his circumstances. Transformation is linked with changed thinking. If you can control what you choose to think about, this will be a major key to you fulfilling your destiny.

Four Keys to Breaking Free from Old Ways

<u>The Jabez Principle</u>:

1. **He encountered the Lord**. The word *called* is the Hebrew word *gara*, meaning to address by name, to cry earnestly unto, to meet, and encounter. Only the presence of God can change your life. You cultivate a hunger for Him when you cry out and seek Him with all of your heart. That hunger will create an opening in your life for the Holy Spirit to transform your life. You must become totally dependent upon the Lord for all your needs. Each one of us must be award of the need for the Lord to bless us in every area of our lives. The Father's blessing drives out all barrenness and brings us into fruitfulness.

2. **He desired that God would enlarge his territory**. The word enlarge is the Hebrew word *rabah*, meaning to increase, multiply, spread, nourish, excel, prosper, to be full in abundance, and to be shot forth. The Lord desires for you to progress into new ground—new ground in your ministry, your walk with Him, your family life, and in many other areas. The Lord wants to bring increase to all, yet many are still waiting for this to take place. You must ask yourself what your motives are for wanting God to enlarge you. Is it your kingdom or His that you are trying to build?

3. **Jabez asked for God's hand**. The hand signifies many things. A man asks for a woman's hand in marriage, which speaks of intimacy and union. God's hand represents the anointing and the presence of God covering us (Exodus 33:22).

4. **Jabez didn't want to remain in his pain**. DON'T ALLOW PAIN TO ATTACH ITSELF TO YOUR PROMISE! Pain will attach itself to your promise, to the point that every time you get close to your promise, pain will rise up and hinder you. Pain comes in many forms:

- Pain of rejection
- Pain of divorce
- Pain of failure
- Pain of mistakes and regrets in life

Pain will rise up every time you get close to your promise and remind you that you have been hurt in life. Don't allow your previous pain to hinder your future.

Jabez became transparent before the Lord, unveiling his present wounds in order to progress into a new place.

But we all with unveiled face beholding as in a mirror the glory of the Lord are being transformed into the same image from glory to glory just as by the Spirit of the Lord.

— 2 Corinthians 3:18

Notice the words "unveiled face." Unveiling one's face speaks of a deep work in man's life, choosing not to remain in darkness, but revealing all to thc Lord. It takes a decision in your heart to break free from your hurts, fears, and inabilities. For example, look at the relationship of the oyster and the pearl. It takes a grain of sand to irritate and cause pain to the oyster before the oyster secretes a fluid that forms into a pearl. There is a pearl in all your pain wanting to come forth if you will unveil all your hurts to your Heavenly Father.

Possessing the Mind of Christ

For my thoughts are not your thoughts.
— Isaiah 55:8

God never said you can't think at His level, but the problem is you choose not to think at His level. When you were born again, you did not receive the "spirit of this world, but the Spirit who is from God," that you might know the thoughts of God. A spiritual man is one in whom the Spirit of God has risen in ascendancy. Paul the Apostle tells us that a spiritual man can discern or appraise all things. God has designed your mind to be a great tool in learning His ways and in walking with Him.

For who has known the mind of the LORD that he may instruct him? But we have the mind of Christ.

—1 Corinthians 2:16

God's Plans are Progressive

Walk in truth:

I have no greater joy than to hear that my children walk in truth.

— 3 John 4

Christianity is about taking hold of truth and progressing forward. Many today have received callings and revelation regarding their destiny, but fail to walk in the truth they have received. There are two categories of people today:

1. Those in defensive mode
2. Those in progressive mode

Both categories of people possess a level of truth. Those living in a defensive mode are people who have received truth yet fail to use this truth to advance in the kingdom. Those who are living in a progressive mode have made the choice to walk in the truth they have. If you fail to walk in the truth you have received, you will never experience the true measure of power that truth can bring into your life. Both groups of people are motivated by a particular belief system.

And Simon Peter answered and said, "You are the Christ, the Son of the living God." And Jesus answered and said to him, "Blessed are you, Simon Barjona: for flesh and blood has not revealed it to you, but my Father which is in heaven. And I say also to you, That you are Peter, and on this rock I will build my church; and the gates of hell shall not prevail against it. And I will give to you the keys of the kingdom of heaven: and whatever you shall bind on earth shall be bound in heaven: and whatever you shall loose on earth shall be loosed in heaven."

— *Matthew 16:16-19*

It's not just the truth you know, it's the truth you apply!

Esther's Example

For if you remain completely silent at this time, relief and deliverance will arise for the Jews from another place, but you and your father's house will perish. Yet who knows whether you have come to the kingdom for such a time as this?

— *Esther 4:14*

Like Esther, you have to make a choice to be part of God's plan or to remain in a place of obscurity. God had planned to deliver the nation of Israel out of the hands of death by using a willing vessel. Esther made the right choice in surrendering to be used by the Lord. You have the privilege today of being used by the Lord; however, one negative thought can prevent you from walking your destiny.

Visionaries Who Chose to Progress in Life

- Drs. William Morton, Horace Wells, and Crawford Long – pioneered the use of anesthesia in surgery in the 1840's.
- Wilbur and Orville Wright – pursued their dream to fly and broke through.

- Alexander Graham Bell – pioneered the invention of the telephone.
- Abraham – believed God and became a Father of Nations.
- David – trusted God's promise and endured to become king.
- Paul – overcame persecution, trials, and sufferings in order to give birth to the ministry of the Gospel to the Gentiles.

Refuse to Allow Your Mind to Limit You in Your Journey

Now to Him who is able to do exceedingly abundantly above all that we ask or think according to the power that works in us.

— Ephesians 3:20

Remember, progression begins with a thought and stakes are loosened by replacing old ways of thinking!

Personal Checklist

1. What things are you meditating upon that are stopping you from progressing?
2. Do you value the truth of God's word and walk in it?
3. Do you think you are on target with the plan God has for your life?

What Changes Do You Need to Make?

- What changes can you make to improve your current state?
- Are you managing your thoughts properly or can you improve?
- Are you spending quality time in the presence of God?

Meditate on These Scriptures

When meditating upon the scriptures, you should speak the Word of God aloud and take the time to slowly think through what you are confessing. By doing so, you are helping to replace old ways of thinking with the Word of God. These scriptures will help strengthen your mind.

You will keep me in perfect peace because my mind is stayed on You.

— Isaiah 26:3

The peace of God, which surpasses all understanding, will guard my heart and mind through Christ Jesus.

— Philippians 4:7

For God has not given me a spirit of fear but of power and of love and a sound mind.

— 2 Timothy 1:7

I set my mind on the things above and not on the things on this earth. I set my mind on the things of God.

— Colossians 3:2

CHAPTER 3

BREAKING FREE OF TEMPTATION

All of you must keep awake (give strict attention, be cautious and active) and watch and pray, that you may not come into temptation. The spirit indeed is willing, but the flesh is weak.

—Matthew 26: 41

A man's disposition on the inside, what he possesses in his personality, determines what he is tempted by on the outside. The temptation fits the nature of the one tempted, and reveals the possibilities of that nature. Every man has the setting of this own temptation, and the temptation will come along the line of the ruling disposition. Temptation yielded to…is a proof that it was timidity that prevented the sin before.

—Oswald Chambers

Hunters often "tempt" ducks or some other kind of bird with a decoy. The real ducks will see them and come in for a closer look. When the curious ducks fly in closer, the hunter shoots them and the hunter's family has duck for dinner. He placed something in front of the birds which excited their curiosity and when they responded naturally, by instinct, the hunter took advantage of that weakness to kill them.

Temptation works in much the same way, and it is the downfall of many good, righteous people. In 1 Corinthians 9:24-27, Paul explains to the brethren that he is not above sin and he even speaks of being disqualified or rejected as a Christian because of this. If that warning were not enough, in chapter 10, he goes on to discuss the Israelites' self-indulgence. He begins by commending them for their faithfulness to God, but in verses 6-10, they become an example for us not to crave things, worship idols, act immorally, try the Lord, or grumble. Paul mentions their behavior as an example again in verse 11, and then finally exhorts the Israelites in verses 12-13.

If any of the Corinthians were feeling arrogant about their strength, Paul told them to remember the Israelites who fell even though they had all those blessings in verses 1-4. Everyone is going to endure temptation, but Paul had some encouraging words for the Corinthians that you can greatly benefit from today.

I. Make Up Your Mind About What it Is

A. Paul described it as a *temptation*. The word means "a testing, trying, or proving." In the Bible, the word is used both in a good connotation (John 6:6; Hebrews 11:17), and in a bad connotation (Matthew 16:1, 22:18; 1 Corinthians 10:9).

B. You need to understand the source of temptation (Matthew 4:3; 1Thessalonians 3:5). Satan is a tempter, but Hebrews 11:17 clearly implies that God also *tries* us in a sense, so when someone speaks of temptation, it is critical to understand the differences between God and Satan.

1. When the Lord *tests* someone, He does it in order to improve them. God does not tempt anyone (James 1:13-16), yet we see Him *testing* His people (1 Peter 1:6-7). God allowed Job to suffer by the hand of the devil in order to demonstrate Job's righteousness and faith (Job 1:8).

2. When Satan *tempts* someone, he does it to cause them to sin (1 Corinthians 7:5; Revelation 2:10). In Matthew 4:1, Satan's purpose was to make Christ sin, thus disqualifying Him for the purpose of redeeming man.

C. When you are being pulled toward sin, realize that you are encountering temptation. Being tempted is not wrong; however, succumbing to temptation is sin.

II. Make Up Your Mind About How it Feels

A. Temptation takes you in its grip, for it has tremendous power. Sometimes people are tempted to commit the same sins over and over in their life; they can never break the cycle. The gospel has the power to save people (Romans 1:16). However, sin also has power, and unfortunately a lot of those who are wrapped up in sin will never break free.

B. Different people have different temptations. For example, drinking a beer has absolutely no tempting effect on me, because I have no desire for it. However, a Christian who used to be an alcoholic may have an extremely difficult time fending off the temptation that does not phase me.

C. James uses the word *entice* in James 1:14. Just like the hunter with a decoy, *to entice* is to catch something with the use of bait. The power of temptation is based upon your desire to do something that is not good for you.

D. Sin seems far from "destruction and perdition" (Hebrews 3:12-13; 1 Timothy 6:9). In fact, the majority of the time seems fun.

E. Some ridicule the Christian way of life and say that they cannot have any fun. Sometimes that is true because their definition of fun goes well beyond ours. You can have fun, but there is a great difference between fun and pushing yourself into temptation.

III. Make Up Your Mind About How it is Experienced

A. Paul described the experience as "common to man." Another version says that it is "the kind that normally comes to man." The word is used in other scriptures to denote *human*. Your temptations are not beyond what you can bear, but you must understand that you will have to bear them.

B. It should be encouraging to understand that your temptations are not greater than anyone else's. Instead of fretting over who has the worst temptation, you can encourage others to put away their sin.

C. In order to make up your mind about how temptation is experienced, you need to explore the different ways you can be tempted:

1. You can be tempted by the threefold nature of sin (1 John 2:16)
2. You can be tempted by a lack of self-control (1 Corinthians 7:5)
3. You can be tempted by being too confident (Galatians 6:3)
4. You can be tempted by a desire for riches (1 Timothy 6:9-10; Matthew 13:22)

5. You can be tempted by getting too close to the wrong crowd (1 Corinthians 15:33)

D. When you are experiencing temptation, you are in good company. Some of the most famous people in the scriptures were tempted:

- Adam and Eve were tempted to eat of the forbidden fruit (Genesis 3:1-6)
- Abraham was tempted to lie to Pharaoh about Sarai (Genesis 12:11-20)
- Moses was tempted to glory in himself (Numbers 20:8-13; Psalm 106:32-33)
- Achan was tempted to take some of the spoils at Ai (Joshua 7:21)
- David was tempted to commit adultery with Bathsheba (2 Samuel 11:1-5)
- Solomon was tempted to turn away from God because of his wives (1 Kings 11:4-8)
- Peter was tempted to deny the Lord three times (Matthew 26:69-75)

E. One great example of encouragement is the temptation of Jesus (Hebrews 2:18). You can take courage because Jesus knows the difficulty of temptation. Although it was terrible that our Lord had to be tempted like a common man, His temptation and strength proved Him to be a worthy Savior, and proved He will care for you in your time of need (Hebrews 4:14-16).

IV. Make Up Your Mind About How to Escape

A. God will give you the way out. You will not have to bear temptations greater than your ability; He gives you the strength to patiently endure temptations which come your way (2 Peter 2:9; 2 Timothy 4:18).

B. If the Lord is faithful enough to provide you a way out of temptation, then you must be wise enough to use it! Although the Lord will not physically come down and keep you from temptation, He does give you ways to escape:

1. When you are being tempted, think about what you are doing. Jesus encouraged His disciples to watch and pray for deliverance from temptation (Matthew 26:41).

2. You also need to flee the scene of temptation (2 Timothy 2:22; Genesis 37:7-12).
3. Whatever tempts you the most, stay away from it (Proverbs 1:10-19).
4. Inform yourself about what Satan is trying to do to you (2 Corinthians 2:11; 1 Thessalonians 3:5; 1 Peter 5:8).
5. Treasure the Word of God in your heart (Psalm 1119:11; Matthew 4:1-11). Use that word to put on the full armor of God (Ephesians 6:10-17).
6. Live by faith in Christ and depend on God's grace (Galatians 2:20; Romans 6:14; 1 John 5:4-5).

C. The surest way of escape is to realize that you need to walk by the Spirit of God and not carry out the desires of the flesh (Galatians 5:16). The Christian has the assurance of God, while the non-Christian is left to battle temptation and sin alone. Mark Twain said, "It is easier to stay out than get out." John Dryden added, "Better shun the bait than struggle in the snare." With all the help and assurance you have, it is not necessary for sin to have dominion over you (Romans 6:7; 1 John 1:7). I wish it could be as easy as speaking the words, but it is not. Unfortunately, almost every day you can hedge yourself into situations where you may compromise your faith. You may think it trivial, but your friends and Satan see it as very significant.

Paul groaned about the struggle between the flesh and the spirit in Romans 7:15-25. He said the members of his body wage war against the law of his mind. In verse 24 he proclaims his wretchedness and in verse 25, he finds the solution. If you hate what you are doing and how you are living because of sin, the only answer is Jesus Christ. The only way to be free from sin is a life in Christ. It is time to lay aside the deeds of darkness and become a new creature.

CHAPTER FOUR

BREAKING FREE FROM GUILT

Perhaps one of the biggest reasons why so many of God's children are living defeated lives is because of guilt. Guilt is one of Satan's biggest weapons against us. It tears us down, it makes us feel dirty and unworthy, and it robs of us of our faith and confidence in Christ Jesus. Jesus not only came to cleanse us from our sins, but also to set us free from the guilt of our sins. If you want to live a life of spiritual victory, you need to have a conscience freed from the guilt of your past.

Holding the mystery of the faith in a pure conscience.
— 1 Timothy 3:9

Two Kinds of Guilt

There are two kinds of guilt described in the Bible. There's Godly sorrow that "leads a person to repentance" (2 Corinthians 7:10), it is known as *conviction*, and it comes from the Holy Spirit. According to John 16:8 (NASB), "When He comes, will convict the world concerning sin." Once a person repents, the guilt lifts and the person feels relieved and joyful that his sins have been forgiven.

Then there's another kind of guilt: condemnation or accusations from the devil. Satan loves to torment God's people by reminding them of their pasts and continually holding their sins before them even after their sins have been forgiven. This is *condemnation* and there is no good that comes out of it whatsoever. It is sent to destroy us, fill us with self-hatred, and rob of us of our faith and confidence in Christ Jesus. It's a lie from the father of lies, and it needs to be ignored.

A lot of believers hear condemning thoughts, and some believers even think it's God telling them these things. My friend, nothing could be further from the truth! God NEVER tells you that you are a loser.

Jesus said He came not to condemn the world, but to save it (John 12:47)!

What is condemnation?

Condemnation comes from Satan and is meant to tear you down. Condemnation continually points out what a failure you are and how badly you've messed up. Condemnation is showing you the problem, but avoiding the solution. Jesus did NOT come to condemn the world (John 12:47). There is no condemnation in Christ Jesus (Romans 8:1). Satan on the other hand is KNOWN for accusing the brethren (Revelation 12:10). Why won't you ever hear God telling you what a failure you are? Because Jesus said, “I came not to judge the world, but to save the world” (John 12:47).

What is conviction?

Conviction is known in the Bible as godly sorrow. God's Word tells us that godly sorrow is what leads us to repentance (Romans 2:4). Condemnation tells you, “You are such a failure! Look at what you did!” On the other hand, conviction tells you, “Come to me and I will forgive you!” Not only is God willing to forgive your sins, but He longs (deeply desires) to do so!

Therefore the LORD longs to be gracious to you, And therefore He waits on high to have compassion on you. For the LORD is a God of justice; How blessed are all those who long for Him.

— Isaiah 30:18 (NASB)

If we confess our sins, he is faithful and just to forgive us our sins, and to cleanse us from ALL unrighteousness.

— 1 John 1:9

Or despisest thou the riches of his goodness and forbearance and longsuffering; not knowing that the goodness of God leadeth thee to repentance?

— Romans 2:4

What is the difference between *Conviction* and *Condemnation*?

Conviction shows you the answer (the Blood of Jesus, which washes away sin), while condemnation shows you the problem (the sin, the past, and your failures). Condemnation shows you the problem, but conviction shows you the answer.

Condemnation shouts, "Your past! Your sins! You loser!" But conviction shouts, "The Blood of Jesus washes away sins! Come to Jesus and be forgiven of your sins! You can be forgiven! Your sins and past don't have to be a part of you anymore!"

Learn what is going on, and stop Satan dead in his tracks. Learn the difference between condemnation and conviction, and stop listening to condemnation. Condemnation comes from the devil, and it's meant to build strongholds in your mind and weaken you spiritually.

Guilt is a Door to the Enemy

Guilt can be an open door used by evil spirits to torment you. False guilt is actually a symptom of unforgiveness in your heart, and is directed at yourself. In Matthew 18:23-35, Jesus tells us how important it is to forgive those who have wronged us, and how we can be turned over to the tormenters (evil spirits) if we have an unforgiving heart.

Colossians 3:13 tells us that we should be people who are "forgiving [of] one another." The phrase *one another* in the New Testament Greek translates to the word *heautou*, which includes one's own self! Bitterness, regardless who or what it's about, defiles a man (Hebrews 12:15). Spiritual defilement is what makes a person open to unclean spirits. It is very possible for a person to be harassed by evil spirits or to come under their power just because a person has refused to forgive himself.

How Guilt is Cultivated and Nurtured

Guilt is cultivated when you continually allow yourself to dwell and think about how badly you've messed up, your past, the sins you've committed, etc. The enemy loves to remind us of our past failures, so he can keep us thinking about them. The problem is, if we allow ourselves to fall for this trap, it allows the enemy to build a stronghold in our minds.

The Stronghold of Guilt

When a person who has repented of their sin(s) but continually feels guilty day after day, even after being told that his past has been washed away and his sins have been forgiven, that person is facing a stronghold. A stronghold is a lie that is believed, which results in an incorrect thinking pattern. The stronghold of guilt is often not alone; it is usually accompanied with an incorrect perception of oneself or an incorrect perception of God (which are both strongholds in themselves).

People who have a stronghold of guilt rarely see God for who He really is (including His awesome forgiving nature) or they don't see themselves correctly. They are new creations in Christ whose pasts have been washed away (2 Corinthians 5:17), but they simply don't believe it because they have strongholds in their minds that need to be torn down.

What is a Stronghold?

A stronghold is a faulty thinking pattern based on lies and deception. Deception is one of the primary weapons of the devil, because it is the building block for a stronghold. What strongholds can do are cause us to think in ways which block us from God's best. For example, if you think you have to confess all your sins to everybody you've ever wronged, you'll feel just awful and guilty until you do all that, and even then, you'll probably still feel guilty, because you will probably forget many people to whom you didn't confess your sins. This is all unnecessary and a waste of time, all because you were deceived and thought that you had to do something that you really didn't have to do.

Here's an example of a stronghold at work: a precious soul is scared of God, and consequently has a hard time feeling His love and presence. He or she views God as a cruel taskmaster, and not as the loving God who is really merciful and gracious to them; therefore, he or she puts up a wall which makes it hard for him or her to receive God's love, presence, and to draw closer in his or her relationship with Him.

If you saw your spouse as a rude and cruel dictator, you probably wouldn't be as apt to snuggle up to Him and love him as you would if you saw him as a loving and kind person who loves you and cares for you. If you see somebody as mean, it's hard to receive his love, isn't it? That's how our perception of God can hinder us from feeling His love and presence in our lives. It is VERY important to have a correct perception of God if we want to live victorious lives in Christ Jesus!

Two Very Destructive Strongholds

<u>When You See God Incorrectly</u>

One of the most common and devastating strongholds to have is an incorrect image in your mind of who God is and how He sees us. People who see God as a taskmaster, live their lives with an unhealthy fear of God. There's a good kind of fear of God, which is more like a holy respect for Him, but there's another kind of fear that is very unhealthy. The enemy wants us to have the kind of fear where we see God as a taskmaster—cruel, cold, distant, uncaring, and ready to snap the whip at us the moment we step out of line.

People who are afraid that they've committed the unpardonable sin are almost guaranteed to have this stronghold. People who find it hard to feel God's love and presence often have this stronghold too. If you feel God is distant and cold, or question if God loves you, then you need to tear down this stronghold.

<u>When You See Yourself Incorrectly</u>

People who suffer from this have a hard time seeing the new person that they are now in Christ Jesus, and often suffer from low self-esteem. They don't understand what Christ did for them, and how it applies to their own lives. Common symptoms of this stronghold are: guilt feelings (questioning if you've really been forgiven of your sins[s]); low spiritual esteem (they feel like sinners, not saints); lack of spiritual confidence that we are supposed to have in Christ Jesus; continual struggles with sin (Jesus said that if you keep in His Word, which tears down strongholds, you will be free from the power sin has over you [John 8:31-34]), and; feeling unworthy spiritually and lacking the joy of the Lord in your life.

How to Tear Down a Stronghold

For the weapons of our warfare are not carnal, but mighty through God to the pulling down of strong holds.

— 2 Corinthians 10:4

Strongholds are birthed and dwell in deception (which are lies and false beliefs), so naturally the cure is to bring the truth of God's Word on to the scene. You debunk the lies of the enemy with the truth, which is in the Word of God! The Bible says that our weapons are mighty for tearing down strongholds in 2 Corinthians 10:4: "For the weapons of our warfare are not carnal, but mighty through God to the pulling down of strong holds." What is our primary offensive weapon? The sword of the Spirit, which is the Word of God (Ephesians 6:17: "...the sword of the Spirit, which is the word of God…").

Truth dispels deception and lies, and therefore the more truth you bring into a situation, the more quickly the darkness will flee. This is where it's important to grow in God's word, because it is your primary weapon for tearing down the strongholds of deception that the enemy has been feeding you. In John 8:31-36, Jesus tells us that we can be held in bondage due to strongholds in our lives. His solution was to "continue in my word... and ye shall know the truth, and the truth shall make you free" (v. 31-32). Strongholds are torn down as we meditate on God's word, which is truth!

If a stronghold of guilt exists, that stronghold needs to be torn down by the renewing of your mind (Romans 12:2). A great place to start is learning how to recognize condemnation from the devil, and stop paying attention to it. You need to know how to recognize the difference between *condemnation* and *conviction.* Once you know the difference between condemnation and conviction and can recognize condemnation when it's thrown at you, you need to guard your thoughts, and when you see condemnation coming your way, pay no attention to it. Treat it for what it really is: a lie from the devil.

Guilt is a Belief

Guilt at its core is a belief—a conviction that we have done wrong and must suffer for it. The only way to break that conviction is to change what we choose to believe. Here are some choices that can help you get the upper hand over guilt.

1. **Choose not rehearse guilt**. Do you find yourself repeating the same guilty thoughts over and over again? They won't go away by themselves. You must choose to make them stop. First, catch yourself. When you find yourself wandering down that painful mental path, put up a mental stop sign. Then deliberately focus on something else, such as your plans for tomorrow. Focusing on something positive in the future is a conscious reminder that there is more to your life than negative experiences from the past.

2. **Choose to accept what cannot be changed**. A self-imposed "penance" for past mistakes accomplishes nothing. It doesn't change or make up for the past; it simply ruins your future. Can you undo what was done? Can you change the outcome of your actions? If the answer is "No," then choose to accept that answer. Accept that the only thing you can change now is your future.

3. **Choose balance**. Guilt keeps us focused on the times we imagined we failed and blinds us to all the other positive and successful times in our lives. So the next time your mind drifts unto those unhappy thoughts, choose to refocus. Force yourself to remember what went right in your life. Recognize that there is – and always have been – a balance between your failures and your successes. No, you weren't 100% perfect, but neither were you 100% flawed.

4. **Choose God's love**. A relationship with God is like no other relationship you may have experienced. God has a unique kind of love for you. It is unconditional (not based upon meeting certain conditions). God love you because He loves you.

In this the love of God was made manifest among us, that God sent his only Son into the world, so that we might live through him. In this is love, not that we loved God but that he loved us.

— 1 John 4:9-10

He does not love you based upon your performance. There is nothing you can do to cause God to love you any more than He already does, and there is nothing that will cause God to love you any less. He loves you, even more than you love yourself.

Know the Difference between Good Guilt and Bad Guilt

Guilt is not necessarily a bad thing unless we carry it after we've been forgiven. Guilt can be a good thing. If it were not for guilt, we would not have turned to Christ for mercy and help. It is a normal response to our conscience. It is better to feel guilty when we do something wrong than to have our conscience seared so that we don't feel anything.

Shame is how we feel about ourselves and what we have done, or how we feel about the things that have happened to us, like sexual violation, etc. It is how we see ourselves. According to Daniel 9:7-8, shame is like a covering over our face. According to Ezra 9:6, when we have shame, we have trouble looking others in the eye. Shame is also reinforced from childhood. We hear things like, "Shame on you." "I'm ashamed of you," and "You ought to be ashamed of yourself" as children, then grow up with a sense of needing to hang our head in shame.

Condemnation is the accusing voice of the enemy telling us how bad and how unworthy we are. Satan will never miss an opportunity to do that. Condemnation comes from the enemy, not from God. Condemnation is intended to push us down and to make us feel defeated and unworthy of God's love, mercy, and grace.

Conviction comes from God. It is accompanied by a sense of wrong, but it always invites us to come back up to where God is. It invites us to seek and receive forgiveness and reconciliation. That is the work of the Holy Spirit. He will never condemn us; He will always convict. The definition of the word *repent* is: to come back to the place you belong. *Pent* is part of the word *penthouse* which is on the upper story—the upper position. To *repent* is to come back up where we belong.

The enemy wants us to feel bad and unworthy. If we've been abused or violated, he wants us to feel like we are damaged goods, like we're not worthy of God's attention, and like we should be embarrassed about ourselves. He wants us to hide ourselves from God and others. Remember Adam and Eve? When they sinned they hid from God. That's what shame wants us to do, hide from God, hang our heads, and cover our faces. Jesus died on the cross, taking all our sin, our guilt, and our shame upon Himself, that we would not have to carry it any longer.

Pray This Prayer:

Father God,

I repent of doubting your love for me. I also repent of not believing that you really have forgiven me and that the blood of Jesus cleanses me from all of the sin, all of the guilt, and all of the shame of my past. Holy God, I repent of listening and agreeing with the voice of the accuser telling me I am an evil person and that I am unworthy to come and receive your love.

I, now in the Name of Jesus, renounce guilt and shame. I renounce condemnation, self–condemnation, and all sense of unworthiness. I renounce every spirit assigned to work against me with guilt, shame, and condemnation. I renounce what they have done to keep me from becoming the person You've created me to be.

I break all agreements I have made with the lying voices of guilt, shame, condemnation, and self-condemnation. I break all word curses I have spoken about myself. I break all soul ties and all generational ties that would bind me in any way to past guilt, shame, and condemnation. I break every vow and covenant, every agreement, and all word curses that would give these spirits any power or influence in my life.

Guilt, shame and condemnation, I break your power over me in the mighty name of Jesus.

Father God, I choose to open my heart right now to receive your unconditional love. I choose to receive your full forgiveness and release from all guilt, shame, condemnation, and sense of unworthiness in my life.

In Jesus' name, amen.

CHAPTER FIVE

BREAKING THE POWER OF REJECTION

The Spirit of the Lord is on me, because he has anointed me to preach the gospel to the poor; he has sent me to heal the brokenhearted, to preach deliverance to the captives, and recovering of sight to the blind, to set at liberty them that are bruised.

— *Luke 4:18*

Five Foundational Aspects of Jesus' Ministry

When you begin to read Luke 4:18, you immediately notice that this is a prophecy God gave the prophet Isaiah concerning JESUS. When JESUS stood up the read from the book of Isaiah, He was reading a prophecy about Himself. There are five foundational points of JESUS' ministry described in Luke 4:18:

1. **Salvation**
Preach the gospel and proclaim the acceptable year of The Lord.
2. **Spirit Baptism**
The Spirit of The Lord is on me and He has anointed me.
3. **Healing**:
Recovering of sight to the blind.
4. **Deliverance**:
Deliverance to the captives.
5. **Liberty**:
Heal the broken hearted and set at liberty those who are bruised or oppressed.

God Anointed Jesus with the Ministry of Release and Liberty to Set People Free

The word *liberty* means "to be free from restrictions and control; free from captivity or restraints; to be released." The ministry of Jesus was and is a ministry of release and liberty. He has been anointed to set the captives free, but He also heals the brokenhearted. Broken people are oppressed people. Broken people are shattered people. For example, if you dropped a glass jar on a concrete floor, it would break into hundreds of pieces, so broken that it couldn't be repaired. But the ministry of Liberty that God anointed JESUS with can put broken, shattered lives back together again.

Jesus Heals Broken Hearts

- Hearts that are broken by sin
- Hearts that are broken by disappointment
- Hearts that are broken by divorce
- Hearts that are broken by betrayal
- Hearts that are broken by rejections

Jesus Can Put Broken Hearts Back Together Again!

A broken heart – if not healed – can open doors to the enemy. When you open the door to the enemy, negative things walk right into your life. If you don't allow Jesus to heal your brokenness, you open the door for anything the devil has for you. Satan loves to traffic in those areas of broken, bruised, and oppressed lives. Because a broken heart and oppressed spirit is fertile ground; it's an open door for a spirit of rejection to walk right into your life. Close the door to the enemy!

In Hosea 8:3 it states, "Israel has rejected the good, the enemy will pursue him." In other words, the enemy pursues or chases you when you are not pursuing the right way. If you disregard God's healing for your brokenness, the enemy will chase you.

Satan Chases After Shattered, Broken Hearts

Satan will chase you down and put into your shattered, broken-to-pieces heart "A SPIRIT OF REJECTION." Let me define *rejection*. Rejection is a feeling of being unaccepted, unwanted, unworthy, left out, and turned away.

- Rejection leaves you with a constant feeling of failure and feeling unaccepted!
- Rejection can destroy a person's life, because it's a spirit of anti-Christ sent to oppose the very nature that God created in you.

- Rejection starves a person from love and acceptance that he was designed to receive.
- Rejection steals your true identity and makes you believe a lie about yourself.

All of Us Have Felt Rejection

Jesus felt rejection: "He came to his own and His own received him not" (John 1:11).
Isaiah 53:3 delves even deeper to describe Jesus' rejection: "He is despised and rejected of men; a man of sorrows, and acquainted with grief: and we hid as it were our faces from him; he was despised, and we esteemed him not." However, there was a purpose to His rejection. Jesus experienced rejection so we could be healed and rescued from a *Spirit of Rejection.*

Satan chases after people whose hearts have been shattered through pain, divorce, failure, being overlooked in life, etc. in order to convince them that their situations are un-repairable.

Why Does Rejection Wound Us So Deeply?

Rejection hurts so deeply because it attacks the very person we are. It destroys our self-esteem and attacks who we are and our purpose in life. This is why it is one of the most common tools the devil will use to destroy a person's life. God never wanted us to feel rejected or abandoned. God desires for you to know who you really are and realize how deeply He loves, accepts, and appreciates you, so that you can live out the fullness of all God has ordained you to be.

God's Word tells us that without being rooted and grounded in the love (and acceptance) of God, we cannot experience the fullness of God in our lives:

And to know the love of Christ, which passeth knowledge, that ye might be filled with all the fullness of God.

— Ephesians 3:19

Rejection has a way of destroying a person's life in a way that few things can. The sad fact is that the number of people who are affected by rejection is staggering. If we want to be all that God has created us to be, then overcoming rejection and its effects is vital and absolutely essential.

The Fruit of Rejection

Many people who have faced rejection and abuse as children grow up with unresolved emotional wounds. Rejection causes emotional wounds which, if not cleansed and released, will grow and fester into spiritual wounds (such as unforgiveness, envy, blaming God, jealousy, etc.). Those spiritual wounds open us up to evil spirits which love to take advantage of this opportunity to invade us. The goal of the enemy is to get us built up with emotional baggage and negative feelings in our hearts against one another, ourselves, and God.

Rejection has a lot of fruit which can vary widely from one person to another. Some of the common symptoms of rejection include:

- Fabricated personalities (being somebody you aren't, in order to be accepted)
- The tendency to reject others, so that you aren't the first one to be rejected
- A tendency to always wonder if a person rejects or accepts you
- The need to fit in or be accepted by others and be a part of everything.
- Self-pity: when people feel bad for themselves because they are alone all the time
- The inability to be corrected or to receive constructive criticism

Rejection Creates an Environment Where You are Starved for Love

Rejection creates an environment where you are starved for love or just don't fit in. You are then in a situation where you may develop the following:

- A tendency to blame God ("Why did He give me this nose?" "Why did God make me so short?"
- A sense of pride that says, "How dare they reject me!"
- An opinionated personality and the need to always be right
- Feelings of worthlessness, insecurity, or hopelessness
- The need to constantly seek a parent's approval, because you base your identity on what they think of you
- Envy, jealousy, and hate for others who are accepted while you are not
- Fear of confrontation (because your identity is based on what others think of you)

People who have a hard time admitting they are wrong, or receiving constructive criticism have an underlying problem with rejection. How do we know that? Because they are basing their identity and who they are upon their ability to be right about everything. Stubbornness can also be rooted in rejection as well for this same reason. They have to be right, or else they feel worthless, because who they are (their identity) is based upon them being right. This also ties in with opinionated personalities, who are always there to tell you all about something, even if they have little or no real understanding of the subject.

Then there are those who are driven by performance orientation or certain variances of OCD, etc., which indicates they are basing their identity and who they are upon how well they perform at something in life. Whenever we base who we are upon our performance, or being correct about something, and then we fail, it is a blow to our identity.

Those who struggle with rejection can also become what we call *fixers*. A *fixer* is a person who is eager to tell everybody else how they need to do things, but many times have little understanding or experience in such matters. Such a person attempts to be the Holy Spirit in other people's lives, where they have no authority or right to step in. They find their identity in fixing other people's problems, and they love it when people come to them for help or advice.

The truth is that we were created to be loved, accepted, and appreciated. Rejection is a spirit of the anti-Christ because it opposes the very nature that God created in us. Rejection starves a person from love and acceptance that he or she was designed to receive. The problem is that when we turn to others or even ourselves for that love and acceptance, we are setting ourselves up for failure and the damage of rejection. Only God can be trusted as the source of our identity.

Self-Rejection

Self-rejection is another piece to this puzzle. Self-rejection is where people reject themselves. They do not like who they are. This can often lead to self-hate, self-resentment, etc. It is often tied in with the inability to forgive oneself, especially if the person has made mistakes in his life which he deeply regrets. Just as it hurts when others reject us, it can do just as much damage when we reject ourselves.

Perceived Rejection

Then there's *perceived* rejection, where a person perceives something as rejection when it really isn't. For example, you may wonder, "Why is that person not coming over here to talk to me?" That person may not be rejecting you, but may just feel shy at the time in stepping out and meeting you (or anybody else for that matter). People who have the spirit of rejection can have a tendency to perceive rejection everywhere from anyone, because the purpose of a spirit of rejection is to make us feel rejected. A person who feels like God is always angry at them usually has issues of rejection. Perceived rejection can also make a person feel as if God has rejected them. This is a very common scenario we encounter in the deliverance ministry.

A good example of rejection, which caused feelings of envy, jealousy, and even hate to surface in King Saul can be found in 1 Samuel 18:7-11:

And the women answered one another as they played, and said, "Saul hath slain his thousands, and David his ten thousands." And Saul was very wroth, and the saying displeased him; and he said, "They have ascribed unto David ten thousands, and to me they have ascribed but thousands: and what can he have more but the kingdom?" And Saul eyed [literally meaning that he looked with jealousy upon] *David from that day and forward. And it came to pass on the morrow* [the next day], *that the evil spirit from God came upon Saul, and he prophesied in the midst of the house: and David played with his hand, as at other times: and there was a javelin in Saul's hand. And Saul cast the javelin; for he said, "I will smite David even to the wall with it." And David avoided out of his presence twice.*

First we see the women praising David for slaying his ten thousands, but praising Saul for slaying only his thousands. This rejection made Saul angry with David and jealous of him. The very next day, an evil spirit came upon Saul and caused him to become exceedingly angry, to the point of attempting to murder David! Now, there's some ugly fruit that all started with rejection.
However, it wasn't rejection that opened Saul up to the evil spirit, but rather his reaction to his rejection.

The same is true when a person becomes stubborn or rebellious, or has any other ungodly reaction to rejection. The rejection isn't the sin, but their reaction can be a serious sin. This can open the person up to unclean spirits, and lead them down the path of destruction. God's Word puts stubbornness and rebellion, for example, in the same category as witchcraft and idol worship!

For rebellion is as the sin of witchcraft, and stubbornness is as iniquity and idolatry. Because you have rejected the word of the LORD, he has also rejected you from being king.

— 1 Samuel 15:23

The Root of Rejection

The root of rejection is actually incredibly simple: damage from rejection is the result of a misplaced identity. Whenever we base our identity on somebody or something other than what God's Word has to say about us, we make ourselves vulnerable to the damage of rejection. Many of us will base our identity on what our parents, teachers, or friends think of us. This sets a lot of children up for performance orientation bondages later in life, because their parents give them conditional love based on their grades or performance.

What or who defines who you are? Is it your job? Is it what your parents thought or think of you? Is it what your friends think of you? Is it how well you perform in the workplace? How much money you have? Is it how high your grades are? Is it what you think of yourself? Is it how physically strong, fit, or tall you are? When you die, will those things continue to define who you are?

Rejection and rising above rejection is all about identity and what you base your identity upon. The key to overcoming rejection, is to solve your identity problems. Let's say that you are basing your identity on what your mother and father think of you. Now the moment that any hint of disapproval comes from them concerning you, that is going to hurt because they are the source of your identity. Anytime we base our identity on what we think of ourselves or what others think of us, we are virtually trusting that person with our identity.

We are not even capable of truly determining who we are; only God is qualified for that job. That is why it is absolutely vital for us to understand the person that God has made in us, and who we are as new creations in Christ Jesus. We were never made to live apart from God or base our identity on things of this world. When we base our identity upon what the Word of God has to say about us, we will become virtually rejection-proof. We can become immune from the wounds of rejection as long as we are not basing our identity upon what that person thinks of us.

Some Dynamics of Rejection

The closer a person is to you, the deeper his or her rejection can wound you. Authority figures are also able to deeply wound you, because you look up to them and rely upon them. Parents often pass rejection on to their children when they say things such as, "I'll love you when you get good grades." Conditional love causes feelings of rejection and bondages such as performance orientation and obsessive competitiveness.

Whether you love or hate a person doesn't immunize anybody from rejection. You can literally want to kill somebody, but still be affected by his or her rejection. The question is this: are you looking to them for approval? Are you basing your identity upon what they think of you? Does their approval of you give your life meaning and purpose?

A person's age also has a lot to do with his vulnerability to rejection. Children are especially vulnerable to the damage of rejection, because they are still developing their identity and learning about who they are. A lot of damage is done by peers in school. Either you're too short, too tall, too fat, too skinny, or you have brown eyes when you should have blue eyes—you name it, and kids will pick on it!

Insecure children can be very cruel and damage other children through rejection. Why? Their own identities are not based on the right things. They do not know who they really are, or who they are called to be, so they go around putting other kids down to make themselves feel better. If they knew who they were in Christ, it would be an entirely different story! They would seek to edify other kids, and help them find their identities and callings as well.

Is it possible to receive rejection from a child or even grandchild? Yes! Nobody is immune, providing that they are basing their identity on what that other person thinks of them. You can be 100 years old and be damaged by the rejection of a caretaker.

Get Your Identity from God's Word!

As I mentioned earlier, it is vital that we base our identity – who we are – upon what God's Word says about us. When we do that, we become virtually immune from the devastating and hurtful effects of rejection. God promises never to leave or forsake us, so when our identity is based upon what He says of us, we can be assured that we're not going to face rejection from Him.

Let your conversation be without covetousness; and be content with such things as ye have: for He hath said, I will never leave thee, nor forsake thee.

— Hebrews 13:5

So What Exactly Does God's Word Tell Us About Who We Are in Christ?

- Because of God's great love for us, we are adopted into His family [1 John 3:1], and made joint heirs with Christ [Romans 8:17].

- We are made to sit in heavenly places (with authority over all demons, sickness, etc.) with Christ [Ephesians 2:6].

- We are blessed with all spiritual blessings in Christ [Ephesians 1:3].

- We are the righteousness of Christ through faith, thus being made right before God [Romans 3:22].

- We are entitled to a clean conscience before God because of the Blood and can have full assurance of faith when we go before Him [Hebrews 10:22].

- Our sins have been removed from us as far as the east is from the west [Psalms 103:12], and God Himself has chosen not to remember our failures [Hebrews 8:12].

- We are loved with the same love that the Father has for Jesus Himself [John 17:23]!

There's one verse in Psalms that really shines the light on how we can be freed from the devastating effects of rejection: "When my father and my mother forsake me, then the LORD will take me up" (Psalm 27:10).

Overcoming Religious Strongholds

Overcoming religious strongholds is necessary to overcome the effects of rejection. You're not going to settle rejection issues fully until you get it down into your spirit that you are accepted, loved, and appreciated by God. Dealing with religious strongholds is vital to this process, as religion paints God as distant, cold, and impersonal. Bringing your relationship with God into proper perspective is a vital step in the process of overcoming the strongholds of rejection.

Tear Down Strongholds

Tearing down the strongholds of rejection is as simple as merely receiving, with childlike faith, what God's Word has to say about your identity. You are a new creature in Christ, who is called to life, purpose, and meaning in Christ.

Know Your Identity

> *And the Holy Ghost descended in a bodily shape like a dove on him, and a voice came from heaven, which said, You are my beloved Son; in you I am well pleased. — Luke 3:22*

The first words about who Jesus' identity came when the heavens opened up and God declared, "You are my beloved son." Although His identity had been set by God, when Jesus went into the wilderness for forty days, Satan came to him and said in John 4:3, "If you be the Son of God, command this stone that it be made bread."

The last thing God said was, "You are my son," and the first thing the devil said was, "If you are the Son of God." Satan wanted to confuse Jesus concerning who He was but it was too late: Jesus knew who He was. Don't let the devil make you doubt who you are.

Satan is not Your Comforter

And no marvel; for Satan himself is transformed into an angel of light.
— 2 Corinthians 11:14

Now notice this, Satan disguises himself as a comforter, but he is a tormentor. He will masquerade himself as a comforter, telling you that it's alright for you to feel rejected and oppressed. He wants you to base your identity on what other people say about you. Remember, The Holy Spirit is your comforter; Satan is your tormentor.

DON'T COME INTO AGREEMENT WITH THE TORMENTOR,
WHO PRETENDS TO BE THE COMFORTER.

But the Comforter, which is the Holy Ghost, whom the Father will send in my name, he shall teach you all things, and bring all things to your remembrance, whatsoever I have said unto you.
— John 14:26

CHAPTER 6

WHAT ARE YOU HOLDING THAT LIMITS YOU?

What do you carry today? What defines you? What are you holding on to that holds you back and keeps you from being everything God saved you to be?

And the LORD said to him, "What is that in your hand?" And he said, "A rod."

— Exodus 4:2

The context of this verse revolves around the call of Moses to be the deliverer of Israel. He is eighty years old and a fugitive from Egypt (Ex. 2:11-15). He lives with his father-in-law Jethro and keeps Jethro's sheep, (Ex. 3:1). Moses does not appear to be a likely choice for the ministry God has in mind.

When the call of God comes, Moses gives every excuse he can think of to get out of what the Lord has for him to do: (1) He says he doesn't feel worthy (Ex. 3:11-12), (2) He says he doesn't even know God's name (Ex. 3:13-14), (3) He says the people will not believe him (Ex. 4:1-9), (4) He says that he is not good with words (4:10-12), and (5) He says, "Send another" 4:13-17). After all the excuses, Moses finally goes to do what the Lord has told him to do (Ex. 4:18-31).

In the middle of this account, God asks Moses a question. That question is found in Exodus 4:2. It is that question that I want to investigate, because that question and the answer to it have importance for our lives right now. The question is rather simple. It is, "What is that in thine hand?" Moses answered, "A rod."

All he had in his hand that day was a simple shepherd's staff. To Moses, all he had in his hand was a dry, dead stick. That's all it was to him, but in the eyes of God it was so much more than that. It's very important for us to examine this text and see what Moses really had in his hands that day. As we do, we will begin to look at our own lives to see the things we also carry in our hands. I want you to see that just as God used what was in the hands of Moses for His glory, He desires to use the things we carry in our hands as well. "**What is that in thine hand?"**

Moses Held His Personality in His Hand

When Moses said, "A rod," he was referring to his shepherd's staff. This was a stick some six feet long that was used in a variety of ways by the shepherd. It was used to guide, lead, and protect the sheep. It was also used to support the shepherd and help him climb up and down the steep mountain places as he led and looked for his sheep. Most importantly, it was used to defend the flock and the shepherd against the attacks of wild animals and others who would threaten the flock. Moses depended on that rod every day he lived.

That rod identified Moses as a shepherd. When people saw that rod in his hand, they would immediately know who he was! That rod also represented all that Moses possessed. He did not even own the sheep that he kept; they belonged to his father-in-law Jethro. All Moses possessed was the rod. It represented his life, his identity, and his livelihood.

The rod in Moses' hand was a constant reminder that he had never reached his fullest potential in the Lord. Forty years earlier God had moved on Moses' heart to deliver Israel from Egypt (Ex. 2:11-14.). At the time of that call, Moses ran ahead of God and took matters into his own hands. Because of what he did, Moses felt like he had wasted his only opportunity to serve the Lord. Moses had come to believe he was worthy of being no more than a shepherd. That stick told Moses, "You are nothing but a shepherd keeping another man's flock!"

Like Moses, we also hold some things in our hands today. Some of those things are good things and others are evil. Here is a short list of some of the things we hold on to today: the past, some pet sin, some hard feelings over things people have done or said to us, unforgiveness, the sorrows of life, feelings of inadequacy, negativity, talents, natural abilities, and accomplishments.

All of these things, whether they are good or bad, identify us and control our lives. We come to depend on the things we hold in our hands and we may even think we can't live without them. They become an integral part of our lives. Like a shepherd leans on his staff, we lean on the things that we hold in our hands, like our past, our problems, our grudges, our abilities, and our talents. We live for these things and we allow them to define our personality and control our spiritual destiny. We look at some of the things we hold in our hands and believe that those things are all we will ever be. God uses Moses to teach us that we can rise above the things that we hold in our hands, and what we hold in our hand does not have to hold us!

Moses Held His Problem in His Hand

When Moses heard the Lord's question, it must have stabbed his heart. "What is that in thine hand?" was the question. "A rod" was the answer. Moses must have remembered a time when his hands held a scepter instead. Surely his mind went back to those days in the palace in Egypt where he was being trained and educated to be a Pharaoh. He may have remembered a time when he held the world in his hand, and now he has nothing but a dry, dead stick in his hand.

God knew what Moses had in his hand. God was not asking for information; God was asking for instruction. God was asking Moses to carefully consider the thing he held in his hand. In Moses' life, the thing he held also held him! That rod identified Moses and that rod also represented all the problems in his life! That rod reminded him that he used to be a prince. That rod reminded him that he was just a servant. That rod reminded him that he was poor and owned nothing. That rod reminded Moses that his life was filled with vast potential at one time, but now he was merely a has-been, a washed up nobody on the back side of the desert.

All the things I mentioned before have the ability to define us. Our sins, our past, our hurts, and our negative feelings about others all impact who we are and how we relate to those around us. They even determine how we serve the Lord. If I allow the negative aspects of my life to control me, then I will stand in the way of the Lord and His will being done in my life. Even the positive aspects of our lives, like our talents and abilities, become liabilities when we depend on them instead of the Lord. I want to remind you that we are to be controlled by nothing and by no one but the Lord Jesus Christ (Eph. 5:18; Gal. 2:20; Rom. 12:1-2).

What do you have in your hand? What are you clinging to today? Is there some attitude, some activity, or some action that defines your life? The only thing that should identify the child of God is *Christ-likeness* (Phil. 1:21). Paul could honestly say, "For to me to live is Christ." If you made that statement, would it come out of your heart? What do you live for? Whatever it is, it reveals your personality. Whatever it is, it controls your life!

Some people can't even worship because they are filled with bitterness over something someone said or did to them. Some people won't serve the Lord because everything in the church hasn't gone their way. Some people are hindered by their sins and some by their self-righteousness. Others are hindered because they think they are the best at what they do. They are filled with pride over their abilities and their accomplishments. They don't even recognize the fact that their achievements have become liabilities in their lives. **"What is that in thine hand?"**

Moses Held His Potential in His Hand

When Moses objects to God's call on his life in Exodus 4, God uses a series of miracles to teach Moses the truth that God will go with him into Egypt and that God will work through him. First, the rod becomes a serpent and then becomes a rod again (vv. 3-4). Second, Moses' hand becomes leprous and then clean again (vv. 6-8). Third, God tells Moses that he will be able to turn water to blood (v. 9). All these miracles are designed to comfort Moses and teach Israel that Moses is indeed a man sent from the Lord.

Moses is commanded to take the rod and "cast it on the ground." When he does this, it turns into a serpent, and Moses runs from the serpent. This tells us that it was probably not an ordinary snake that Moses might have encountered day by day in the wilderness. Most likely, it was a cobra. Cobras were worshipped as gods by the Egyptians. Pharaoh even wore a golden cobra around his neck. Seeing Moses take a stick and turn it into a cobra would be a commentary to both the Israelites and the Egyptians. It would tell both that the God Moses represented was more powerful than the gods the Egyptians worshipped.

Here's the point: to Moses that rod was nothing but a tool, a weapon, a necessary part of his life. In his hand, it helped support him. It helped protect and guide his flock, and it helped him in many ways day by day. But in his hands it was still just a dead, dry stick. When that stick was given over to the Lord, it became a living thing. It became a thing of power that God used to defeat Israel's enemies and to glorify God. God took that insignificant stick and worked wonders with it.

- It was used to confront the Egyptian soothsayers (Ex. 7:12).
- It was used to turn the waters of Egypt to blood (Ex. 7:17-20).
- It was used to bring forth the plague of frogs (Ex. 8:5).
- It was used to bring forth the plague of lice (Ex. 8:16).
- It was used to bring forth the plague of thunder and hail (Ex. 9:23).
- It was used to call an east wind that blew in the plague of locusts (Ex. 10:13).
- It was used to part the Red Sea (Ex. 14:16).
- It was used to cause the Red Sea to come together again, drowning Pharaoh and his army (Ex. 14:27).
- It was used to bring water from a rock in the desert (Ex. 17:5).

- It was used to bring victory over the Amalekites (Ex. 17:9).

In Exodus 2:4, Moses was commanded to, "Put forth thine hand, and take it [the serpent] by the tail." People who work with snakes will tell you that this is a recipe for disaster. If you are going to pick up a snake, you should always grab it behind the head. Moses was commanded to take the snake by the tail to teach him that he could trust the Lord to take care of him. When Moses obeyed, the serpent became a dead stick once more, but I guarantee you that Moses never looked at that stick the same way again!

God took that stick, that weak, powerless, dead, dry stick and used it in a mighty way, simply because Moses yielded it to the Lord. Had it remained in Moses' hands, it would have held no power for God, but it would have held all power over his life. Because he yielded to the Lord, Moses was freed from its power over him and he was free to use its power for the glory of God.

I do not know what you hold in your hand today. However, I do know this: if what you hold in your hand is not yielded to the Lord, it is a hindrance in your life! It holds you back from being everything you could be for the Lord. Not only does it hold you back, but it also affects everyone around you! It affects your family. It affects your church. It affects everything you touch in your life and everything that touches you.

- That sin you refuse to abandon to the grace of God is a dead stick in your hand; when you give it to God in confession and repentance, it becomes an opportunity for Him to display His grace, His forgiveness, and His restoration.

- That bitterness over some past wrong you feel you have suffered is a dead stick in your hand; when you bring that thing to God, He is able to deliver you from the bondage you are in and restore you to a place of blessing.

- That negative spirit you possess that causes you to look for the bad in everyone and everything is a dead stick in your hand; when you bring it to the Lord, He is able to give you His perspective on people and events. He is able to bring you out of that bondage.

- That sorrow that you have allowed to shape your life and steal your joy is a dead stick in your hand; bring it to God and He will teach you that He has a purpose even in your pain, and He will teach you the truth of Romans 8:28.

- That ability you have that you are so proud of can be a dead stick in your hand; when that ability is surrendered to the Lord, it becomes a channel of blessing whereby He is able to use your life in greater ways.

- Those accomplishments in your past that you continually look to is a dead stick in your hands; when you yield them to the Lord, He will enable you to see that He has even greater things in your future.

Everything we hold in our hands is either a burden or a blessing depending upon what we do with it. When we hold on to it, it is a problem. When we yield it up to the Lord, He is able to release its potential for blessing in our lives. Everything I hold in my hands can hinder my life, my walk with God, my family, and my church if those things are not yielded to the sovereign control of Almighty God.

Sometimes we wonder why God isn't working in the church and saving souls like we think He should be. It may be that there are some people who, like Moses, are holding dead sticks in their hands that need to be surrendered to the Lord. It may be that some are like Achan in Joshua 7:21, "When I saw among the spoils a goodly Babylonish garment, and two hundred shekels of silver, and a wedge of gold of fifty shekels weight, then I coveted them, and took them; and, behold, they are hid in the earth in the middle of my tent, and the silver under it." There is sin buried deep within us that needs to be brought out and dealt with. Moses climbed that mountain that day with a dead stick. He had been carrying around that dead stick for forty years. In all that time, he had used that stick, but that stick had also used Moses.

That stick identified him. That stick controlled his life. That stick said, "All you will ever be is a shepherd keeping another man's sheep." That stick was a problem for Moses and he didn't even realize it. He believed that it was an indispensable part of his life and work. Moses never knew, until he yielded that stick to God, that the stick he held in his hand was the key to God's power in his life. Moses yielded the stick he carried that day to the Lord. When he did, he was released from its power. When he did, it ceased to define him. When he did, it became the power of God in his life.

What are You Holding That Limits You?

What do you carry today? What defines you? What are you holding on to that holds you back and keeps you from being everything God saved you to be? Is there some sin that needs to be laid down? Is there some event from your past, some hurt, some sorrow, some bitterness, that hinders you today? Is there some area of your life where you feel like you have arrived? Is there some talent or ability that fills you with pride? Is there something in your life that holds you back? Is there something in you that holds your family and your church back?

Look at your life and see what you hold. You may hold it in your hand, but it dominates and controls your life. This is an opportunity for you to be free from its pull and from its influence. Throw it down and let God have it. When you hold on to it, it is a liability; when you give it to Him, it becomes a spiritual asset!

LIFE IS EITHER ABOUT A DEAD STICK OR A LIFE OF VICTORY

Life is either about a dead stick or a life of Victory. Bring what you hold in your hands and cast it down before Him. Let Him take that liability and turn it into an asset for His glory.

CHAPTER 7

MOVING PAST YESTERDAY

Until the desire to go forward becomes greater than the memories of past pain, you will be held hostage by the memories of your pain.

God wants to give you the strength to overcome the pain of your past and give you the power to move forward into your destiny. According to Proverbs 29:18, "**Where there is no vision, the people perish.**" *Vision* is simply the desire to move forward or to move ahead. Until you have vision to move forward, you will always live in yesterday's struggles.

God Wants to Put the Desire in Your Spirit to Move Forward

Desire is the evidence that something is there. Desire is the evidence that God has put something in your spirit, because you can't desire something that isn't there. The very fact that you have a desire is in itself an indication that better days are coming!

"I would have lost heart unless I had believed that I would see the goodness of The Lord in the land of the living" (Psa. 27:3). The psalmist's vision or desire to see the goodness of the Lord was greater than his thoughts of giving up. Until the desire to go forward becomes greater than the memories of past pain, you will never hold the power to create again. Your dream will die. Your vision will die. Your hope will die.

For example, when a woman goes into the delivery room to have a baby, there is intense pain, but her desire to give birth to that baby becomes greater than her present pain. It was the desire to give birth to that baby that made her continue. She endured the pain, so new life could be born. However, once the baby is born, the pain will soon be forgotten.

IF THE PAIN OF PAST MEMORIES BECOMES GREATER THAN THE DESIRE TO MOVE FORWARD OR TO GO AHEAD, FEAR WILL DESTROY THE POWER OF CREATIVITY WITHIN YOU.

The enemy wants you to live in yesterday. He wants to draw your attention backwards, on your yesterdays. He tells you what you cannot do and he reminds you of the pain of your past. He will keep you chained to fear; however, you can never receive what God has for you if you continue to look back.

Here is What God Does

God puts something before you that is stronger than your struggles. Your struggles want to pull you back, but God puts something greater and stronger before you. God puts vision before you that is greater than the thing that is drawing us back. The Psalmist is saying, "My desire to see the goodness of God was greater than the thing that was causing me to lose heart."

When my son Larry Jr. was a young boy, he was given a dog that he named Cesar. Cesar was a big, husky dog that we had to keep tied up in the backyard. We had to keep Cesar restrained because he would chase cars and people. One day Cesar saw something that he really wanted. The trash man was picking up our trash early one morning and Cesar was tied up in the back yard. The trash man was out of Cesar's reach, but the motivation before Cesar was greater than the rope that held him back. Cesar pulled that rope until the rope snapped and he was loose to chase what he desired.

God puts something before you that is a stronger desire than your struggles. The thing that used to pull you back will snap and break when you allow God to put a desire in you that becomes greater than the thing that limits you. It happens when the motivation before you becomes greater than the thing behind you. God will cause you to BREAK FORTH. When God causes you to break forth, people can't hold you back. When God causes something to break forth, the devil can't hold it back. When God allows something to break forth, circumstance can't hold it back.

For you shall break forth on the right hand and on the left.
—Isaiah 54:3

1. JOY BREAKS FORTH OUT OF HEAVINESS!
2. LIGHT BREAKS FORTH OUT OF DARKNESS!
3. YOU BREAK FORTH INTO SINGING!

What Will Cause That Kind of Breaking Forth?

This kind of breaking forth happens when you put truth in your spirit and feed it the Word of God. Our problem is this, we starve the seed of faith that is growing within us by what we tell ourselves.

- STOP TELLING YOURSELF THAT YOU ARE A FAILURE
- STOP TELLING YOURSELF THAT YOU ARE IGNORANT
- STOP TELLING YOURSELF THAT YOU ARE TOO OLD
- STOP TELLING YOURSELF THAT IT'S TOO LATE
- STOP STARVING YOUR FAITH BY YOUR NEGATIVE CONFESSIONS

Do You Know It's Unwise to Speak Against Your Body?

When you speak against your body you are opening the door for sickness and diseases. Speak life to your body.

I will praise you, for I am fearfully and wonderfully made; marvelous are your works and that my soul knows very well.

— Psalm 139:14

And the Lord will make you the head and not the tail; and you will be above, and not beneath.

Deuteronomy 28:13

I can do all things through Christ who strengthens me.

Philippians 4:13

Feed the Seed of Faith That is within You

The book of Hebrews gives us a tremendous lesson on faith. Look at Hebrews 11:3:

By faith we understand that the worlds were framed by the Word of God, so that the things which are seen were not made of things which are visible.

Now notice what that verse says, "The invisible became visible and was manifested because of a Word from God."

One Word from God Can Frame Your World!

In Hebrews 11:3, the word *framed* means, "order or to cause it to come to pass." The word *world* in this context means, "time period or a period of time." One word from God can order your life and cause what you can't see to become visible.

The steps of a good man are ordered by the LORD: and he delighteth in his way.

— Psalm 37:23

God Will Cause Your Steps—Your Progression to Come to Pass!

What God wants to do in us begins as a word that gets into our spirit. It was a dream first and then became a reality. It was a thought first and then became visible. Just because you can't see it now, doesn't mean you won't get it.

Let me show you this progression in the Bible characters mentioned in the book of Hebrews Chapter 11. Notice what the Bible says about the faith of Abe and Enoch.

Abel worshipped God by faith.

Verse 4: “By faith Abel offered to God a more excellent sacrifice than Cain, by which he obtained witness that he was righteous, God testifying of his gifts: and by it he being dead yet speaks.?

Enoch walked with God by faith.

Verse 5: “By faith Enoch was translated that he should not see death; and was not found, because God had translated him: for before his translation he had this testimony, that he pleased God.”

Now look at this progression: you can't walk with God until you have worshipped God. We try to walk with God without worshipping Him. If you won’t worship God, you won’t walk with God.

Hebrews 11:4-5 says Abel worshipped God and Enoch walked with God, but the progression continues in Hebrews 11:7: “By faith Noah, being warned of God of things not seen as yet, moved with fear, prepared an ark to the saving of his house; by the which he condemned the world, and became heir of the righteousness which is by faith.”

Now take notice of this progression: (1) Abel worshipped God, (2) Enoch walked with God, and (3) Noah worked for God. You can't work with God, until you walk with God. You can't walk with God, until you worship God. If you can worship like Abel, then you can walk like Enoch. If you walk like Enoch, then you can work like Noah. This progression of faith continues in Hebrews 11:8-12:

v. 8: By faith Abraham, when he was called to go out into a place which he should after receive for an inheritance, obeyed; and he went out, not knowing where he went.

v. 9: By faith he sojourned in the land of promise, as in a strange country, dwelling in tabernacles with Isaac and Jacob, the heirs with him of the same promise:

v. 10: For he looked for a city which has foundations, whose builder and maker is God.

v. 11: Through faith also Sara herself received strength to conceive seed, and was delivered of a child when she was past age, because she judged him faithful who had promised.

v. 12: Therefore sprang there even of one, and him as good as dead, so many as the stars of the sky in multitude, and as the sand which is by the sea shore innumerable.

Hebrews Chapter 11 tells us that faith progresses. Able worshipped by faith, Enoch walked by faith, Noah worked by faith, and Abraham lived by faith. Abraham was a great man of faith. By faith he went out from his country, at God's command, not knowing where he was going. By faith he journeyed into the land of promise. And by faith he looked for a city built and made by God. God gave Abraham many promises regarding his future and his descendants. God told Abraham that his seed would be as the sand on the sea shore and as the stars of heaven.

That in blessing I will bless thee, and in multiplying I will multiply thy seed as the stars of the heaven, and as the sand which is upon the sea shore; and thy seed shall possess the gate of his enemies.

— Genesis 22:17

God told Abraham this before he had his first child. His seed would be as the sand of the sea shore. God was showing Abraham his natural seed, Israel, but God also said Abraham's seed will be as the stars of heaven. God was showing Abraham his spiritual seed, the church.

The only thing between the seed, the sand, and the stars was a woman whose name was Sarah. The Bible says that God gave Sarah "strength to conceive seed" when she was too old to have a child. So you have Abraham an old man, Sarah as an old woman, and a seed.

But God said, "I will give Sarah the strength to conceive and from that seed will come forth descendants as numerous as the stars of heaven and the sand on the sea shore."

Whatever God Gives You, He Wants It to be Multiplied in Your Spirit

When it comes forth it will be greater that the former. Are you ready for God to increase you? Are you ready for God to show Himself strong in your life?

Satan wants to multiply fear in your life. He wants you to become so afraid that you won't be able to figure out what you fear. The enemy chains us to the circumstances of the past to keep us from reaching our potential. The devil wants to destroy the spirit of creativity that is within you. He wants to block your spiritual womb, causing you to be less productive than you want to be. Don't be afraid of the devil's lies. Greater is He that lives within you, than the power that works against you!

God Has Not Given Us a Spirit of Fear

For God hath not given us the spirit of fear; but of power, and of love, and of a sound mind.

— 2 Timothy 1:7

Your fear is driven by reversed thinking. In other words, "what could go wrong in life, as opposed to what could go right in life."

<u>The Seven Levels of Fear</u>

Level 1: Paralysis
Fear of doing the wrong things and consequently doing nothing.

Level 2: Inefficiency
Fear of wasting time. Fear of doing the right things wrong.

Level 3: Catastrophizing
Catastrophizing is an irrational thought a lot of us have in believing that something is far worse than it actually is. It's the fear things will get worse rather than better. Seeing only the worst case scenario.

Level 4: Holding On
Fear of letting go. Focusing on the 80% that only brings 20% of the value to things. Fear that stopping something you're doing will be a mistake. Just-in-case fear: "Let's take everything just to be safe."

Level 5: Self-Doubt
Fear of not being physically able. Fear of not copying the right thing. Fear of copying the right things in the wrong manner. Fear of being laughed at. Fear of criticism. Fear of self.

Level 6: Normalcy
Fear of being different. Fear of being noticed. Fear of being laughed at. Fear of rejection. Fear of tradition. Fear of trying different things that might not work. Fear of failing while trying. Fear of the unexpected. Fear of getting hurt. Fear of exposure.

Level 7: Disbelief
Fear of the unknown. Fear of not having a basis of comparison. Fear of problem size. Fear of believing. Fear that says, "I can't do that." Fear of total failure. Fear of the point of no return. Fear of death and not coming back alive. Fear of others dying. The sum of all fears.

The Seven Levels of Change

Einstein pointed out that "the significant problems we face today cannot be solved at the same level we were at when we created them." To get different results or CHANGE, we must do things differently. The following are the levels in which we can affect change:

Level 1: Effectiveness – DOING the right things
Level 2: Efficiency – DOING things right
Level 3: Improving – DOING things better

Level 4: Cutting – Stop DOING some things
Level 5: Copying – DOING things other people are doing
Level 6: Different – DOING things no one else is doing
Level 7: Impossible – DOING things that can't be done

How Do We Overcome Fear?

1. **Burn the Boats**

The ancient Greek warriors were some of the toughest fighters of the time. It wasn't so much their training or their weapons or their tactics that made them so fierce—it was their unwavering commitment to win. When they would arrive on enemy shores, the first orders from their commanders would be to "Burn the boats." And they would torch their boats. The message was loud and clear: there was no turning back, no retreat, and no surrender. The only way out was forward. Victory or death. There was no other outcome. Don't give yourself a reason to fail or fear —"Burn the boats!"

2. **Take Action**

Taking action begins by questioning where you are. How did I get to place of fear in my life? You will never move out of your fear until you begin to question how you got there. Questions lead to exploring options. Lay out all the options of how to break free from this fear. Once you have laid out all the options, choose the best option. The best option is to first give it to God. Options lead to open doors. You will never know the door that God will open for you until you question where you are, how you got there, and look at your options to free yourself from this fear. Then watch God open doors that you didn't know were possible.

3. **Surrender the Outcome**

We are afraid to take a risk because the outcome is not guaranteed. By faith plant the seed, water the seed, and let things develop in their own way and time. God didn't say you had to create the harvest. He said if you will do your part and plant the seed and water the seed you have planted, God will take care of the outcome.

4. Don't Stop at the Tipping Point!

Let me explain this by using an example of pushing a car up a hill. If your car has ever broken down in a low place and the only place to get it repaired is over the next hill, you may have to push it over that hill. When you push anything up a hill, gravity begins to work against you. But once you reach the center of gravity or the tipping point (the place where the weight is evenly dispersed and all sides are in balance), the car can go either way, because you have it at the tipping point. The thing that worked against you, pushing you back, is now working for you. You have reached the tipping point. You have reached the place of no going back.

Now the thing you've been pushing with all your might has reached the tipping point and no more pushing is required. Your faith will give you the ability to push your way through difficult seasons of life, until you reach the tipping point. Now let your faith work for you and take you where you need to be.

CHAPTER 8

TURN THE PAGE

One of the most difficult things we deal with in life is not change, but *transition*. Transition is the process of letting go inwardly of what was. It is the process of letting go of "***what was***" to take hold of ***what is becoming***, and then recognizing that it's just another chapter in the story of our lives.

It's the Process of Turning the Page

Life is filled with changes, but transition is different than change.

- Change is what life becomes.
- Change is the end result.
- Change is the next chapter of your life.
- Transition is the process of turning the page. It is the process of letting go of what was or the way things used to be in order to take hold of the way things have become.

Many of you are already in the process of a transition in your life; you are leaving one thing to get to another thing. You are in the process of moving from one season of life to the next. For example:

1. Turning the page from being single to being married.
2. Turning the page from being a teenager to becoming an adult.
3. Turning the page from one career in life to another career.
4. Turning the page from fulltime employment to retirement.
5. Turning the page from being a couple to having children.
6. Turning the page from having children in the house to an empty nest.
7. Turning the page from being young to growing older.

Transition is turning the page!

When You Turn the Page, You Begin to Ask Questions:

What will happen next?
What will I do?
Who will I be?
Who am I now?

When you turn the page and go to the next chapter of your life, the rules you were once accustomed to change.

For the priesthood being changed, there is made of necessity a change also of the law.

— Hebrews 7:12

How do You Move from What was, to What is to Become?

1. **Start by leaving the previous chapter.**

Your life is an unfolding story filled with many chapters. When you come to the end of one chapter, that's not the end of the story; there is another chapter that unfolds. You have to turn the page or you will never get to the next chapter of your life. Face it, you can't stay in the previous chapter of your life. It may have been a good chapter, but when it ends, it ends. Time has a way of always moving us forward.

Nothing stays the same!

For example, Israel was in transition, but they could not turn the page. The children of Israel were in Egyptian bondage and enslaved for over 400 years. They cried out to God for change, so God sent them a deliverer.

Moses led them out of Egyptian bondage toward the Promise Land, but first they had to cross the Red Sea. However, before they could even cross the Red Sea, they wanted to go back to Egypt. And three days later after they had crossed the Red Sea, they still wanted to go back to Egypt.

The children of Israel had ten windows of faith that opened to them to trust God and believe God to get them to the Promise Land, but they could never turn the page. They never let go of the past!

- Their past world was Egypt
- They walked like Egyptians
- They talked like Egyptians
- They ate Egyptian food
- They even thought like the Egyptians

They wanted to go back to Egypt because they were unwilling to turn the page. They could never envision their future story; they were stuck in the past. When you are stuck in past, you can't see your future. God worked miracles for them, but they wanted to go back. God made their shoes last for forty years so their feet would not get used to the desert sand and call it the Promise Land, but they wanted to go back to Egypt.

You will always go back to what you are connected too! You've got to leave that chapter of your life behind, as Paul writes in Philippians 3:13: "Forget what lies behind and pressing or straining forward to what lies ahead."

This verse tells me that Paul struggled with turning the page: "Putting those things behind me I press toward to mark of the high calling."

What did Paul have to put behind him? He was educated, a Pharisee, and he excelled at everything, but God called him in a different direction. Paul left the previous chapter of his life to follow the will of God. He turned the page and opened the next chapter.

2. <u>Turn to the next chapter.</u>

You can't start the next chapter of your life if you keep re-reading the last chapter. When Moses died, the children of Israel could not get past that chapter. Moses died and they could not turn the page. Therefore, God allowed the children of Israel to mourn for thirty days. However, after that time, God told Joshua – their new leader – to tell the people to get ready, because in three days they would cross the Jordan. They had to move on; they had to turn the page.

Look at Matthew 14:29-30 which details the night Simon Peter walked on the water. This was truly a miracle: he walked on the very thing that tried to drown him. Simon Peter walked on the water, but when he took his eyes off Jesus and focused on the wind, he started to sink. Verse 30 says, "But when he saw that the wind was boisterous, he was afraid; and beginning to sink he cried out, saying, 'Lord, save me!' "

He saw the wind which represents *spirit*. Peter was overcoming the wind that worked against his faith, but when he took his eyes off JESUS and looked at the boisterous spirit that was working against him, he started to drown in the thing he had just overcome.

However, he cried out to Jesus and said, "Lord save me!" He turned the page. Simon Peter would have never been the great apostle that he was if he had kept reading that chapter of his life when he lost his faith.

TURN THE PAGE!

You can't change your past, but you can turn the page and go to the next chapter of your future.

How Do You Turn the Page?

1. **Recognize your ruts.** A rut is a long deep track made by the repeated passage of the wheels of vehicles. A rut is also a habit or

pattern of behavior that has become unproductive, but is hard to change.

- Don't get stuck in the ruts of life.
- Don't get stuck in deep ruts of life that you can't get out of.
- Don't get stuck between the chapters of your life in ruts where you can't turn the page and go to the next chapter.

2. **Clean up your lenses.** The road to change may be right in front of you, but you can't see it because your life lenses are blurred or dirty.

3. **Eliminate self-sabotage.** You are your biggest enemy! Most of the time we aren't fighting the devil; we are fighting our own insecurities:

a. fear of failure
b. fear of not measuring up
c. feeling like you are not good enough
d. believing that change is impossible

All of these mindsets are forms of self-sabotage. Thinking that change is impossible is a form of self-sabotage.

4. **Realize there are some things in life you have no control over.**

- Weather/traffic
- Other people's opinion of you
- Crazy life stuff that just happens

Don't let what is out of your control interfere with all the things you can control.

5. **Realize every step is necessary.** We learn from every step we take. Whatever you do today is a necessary step to get you to tomorrow. You may not be as good as you want to be today, but thank God for all the lessons you've learned along the way.

6. Let the lessons of life make you better, not bitter! In John 5:2-9, the man at the pool of Bethesda is a man waiting without hope. He lost his expectation in the process of time. Don't lose your hope while you wait for your miracle.

The Bible teaches that there are three things that will remain forever: Faith, Hope, and Love. Faith is always in the now. Hope is always in the future. Faith is the sail on the ship and hope is the wind that blows us into our destiny.

CHAPTER 9

CONFESS AND POSSESS

Make These Your Breakthrough Confessions Today:

I confess Jesus as my Lord (Rom. 10:9-10); I possess salvation.

I confess, "By His stripes I am healed" (Is. 53:5); I possess healing.

I confess, "The son has made me free" (Jn. 8:36); I possess absolute freedom.

I confess, "The love of God is shed abroad in my heart by the Holy Ghost" (Rom. 5:5); I possess the ability to love everyone.

I confess, "The righteous are bold as a lion" (Pr. 28:1); I possess lion-hearted boldness in spiritual warfare.

I confess, "He will never leave me nor forsake me" (Heb. 13:5-6); I possess the presence of God with each step I take.

I confess, "I am the redeemed of the Lord" (Ps. 107:2); I possess redemption benefits every day.

I confess, "The anointing of the Holy One abideth in me" (1 Jn. 2: 27); I possess yoke-destroying results by this anointing (Is. 10:27).

I confess, "In the name of Jesus I can cast out devils" (Mk.16:17); I possess dynamic deliverances to overcome the devil.

I confess, "I lay my hands on the sick and they shall recover" (Mk. 16:18); I possess positive healings for the oppressed.

I confess, "I am a branch of the Living Vine" (Jn. 15:5); I possess Vine Life wherever I go.

I confess, "I am the righteousness of God in Christ" (2 Cor. 5:21); I possess the ability to stand freely in God's holy presence and in Satan's presence as a victor!

I confess, "I am a temple of the living God" (2 Cor. 6:16); I possess God dwelling in me and walking in me!

I confess, "My God shall supply all my need" (Phil. 4: 19); I possess the supply of every need in my life. It is met in Jesus' name!

I confess, "For whosoever shall call upon the name of the Lord shall be saved" (Rom. 10:13); I possess know-so salvation for I have called upon the name of the Lord.

I confess, "The Lord shall preserve me from all evil" (Ps.121:7); I possess preservation from all forms of evil.

I confess, "Blessed are the pure in heart: for they shall see God" (Mt.5: 8); I possess the assurance I shall see God for the blood of Jesus has made me pure in heart.

I confess, "The Lord will give strength unto His people; the Lord will bless His people with peace" (Ps. 29:11); I possess daily strength and an abundance of peace.

I confess, "Blessed be the Lord, who daily loads us with benefits" (Ps. 68:19); I possess a life daily loaded with the benefits of the Lord.

I confess, "I am the light of the world: he that follows Me shall not walk in darkness, but shall have the light of life" (Jn. 8:12); I possess light upon life's pathway for I am following Jesus.

I confess, "And God is able to make all grace abound toward you; that ye, always having all sufficiency in all things, may abound to every good work" (2 Cor. 9:8); I possess all grace: abounding grace, saving grace, healing grace, baptizing grace, and all-sufficient grace.

I confess, "For with God nothing shall be impossible" (Lk. 1:37); I possess impossibilities becoming realities, for I am linked up with God by divine birth.

I confess, "I will pour out of my Spirit upon all flesh" (Acts 2:17); I possess the Spirit outpoured upon my life continually.

I confess, "As far as the east is from the west, so far hath He removed our transgressions from us" (Ps.103:12); I possess the assurance that my sins are removed far from me. Hallelujah!

ABOUT THE AUTHOR

J. Larry Gunter

In 1998, J. Larry Gunter was appointed senior Pastor of Victorious Life Church in Conyers, Georgia. Immediately God put a dream in the heart of the Pastor to build a Multicultural church without racial, national, cultural, or color barriers. In October of 2008, another dream was realized when the Victorious Life congregation moved into a new sanctuary. Under the Leadership of Pastor Gunter, Victorious Life has experienced exponential growth with present membership reaching 1200.

J. Larry Gunter and his wife Kathleen grew up in southern Georgia as Southern Baptists. They both have been active in ministry as Pastor and Evangelist. The calling of God has taken Pastor Gunter around the world preaching the gospel. He presently conducts conventions annually in Jamaica, as well as in the country of Namibia, Africa, where he helps oversee a large ministry called *Christ Love Ministries*. Larry and Kathleen are the parents of two children, and have four grandchildren. Pastor Gunter attended Truett McConnell College and is a graduate of Beulah Heights University.